PRAISE FOR *BLENDING LEADERSHIP*

"*Blending Leadership* combines detailed research with narrative familiar to every educator as the authors explore and explain the rapidly evolving arena of leadership in a digital age. . . . As our school organizations become increasingly fluid and evolutionary, the effective leader will leverage technical literacy and abilities in ways that will amplify the effectiveness of our collective mission of great learning for each individual student. The book, written by co-authors with extensive experience in the trenches of great learning, brings to light opportunities for this leverage for teachers, administrators, and students across every facet of our schools."

Grant Lichtman, author of *#EdJourney:
A Roadmap to the Future of Education

"In *Blending Leadership*, authors Valentine and Richards encourage independent school leaders to take a 'design pause' by using greater intention in how they communicate and collaborate. At a time when we all need to challenge our traditional thinking and the status quo for doing business as 21st century independent schools, *Blending Leadership* offers practical examples that demonstrate how independent schools have the potential to serve as catalysts for the very conversations we need to have the most."

Jeffrey Shields, president and CEO,
National Business Officers Association (NBOA)

"This book captures the iterative exploration of Stephen Valentine and Reshan Richards as they seek to show how leadership really works. Sketchnotes by Brad Ovenell-Carter add a rich, visual dimension that create an engaging guide for a new generation of learners."

Mike Rohde, author of *The Sketchnote Handbook* and
The Sketchnote Workbook

"*Blending Leadership* comes at the perfect time for today's digital leaders. The title captures the opportunities and challenges of leadership and the book recognizes that technology is not a zero sum

game. Successful approaches to digital leadership in today's schools are not binary. With colorful examples and lively metaphors, *Blending Leadership* is a practical guide that today's school leaders will call upon over and over again."

Matt Levinson, head of school, University Prep, and author of *From Fear to Facebook: One School's Journey*

"With riveting storytelling, Reshan and Steve tell the stories of K-12 educational leaders who are thriving in online, offline, and blended environments. A mix of theory and practical ideas, the text encourages you to make both big changes and small tweaks to the ways you communicate and organize learning."

Dr. Kristen Swanson, cofounder of the Edcamp Movement

"In the expertly crafted *Blending Leadership,* Valentine and Richards, along with the phenomenal sketchnotes of Ovenell-Carter, treat the reader to an insightful look at the ways that leaders can truly embrace a culture shift to become even more effective. The book offers deep examples that are well referenced and researched and has many anecdotes that help put the concepts into context. The practical suggestions of implementation are scaffolded and varied in their approach. This is leadership in practice as well as a must-read for educators everywhere."

Adam Bellow, educational technologist and founder of eduTecher/eduClipper

"Valentine and Richards have created a practical technology-blended roadmap for school leaders in their book. With stories of successful practices, validation from leadership experts, and ideas on how to use technology effectively in a leadership role, their book is a must-read for administrators and aspiring administrators!"

Kathy Schrock, educational technologist, kackl! and adjunct faculty, Wilkes University

"In *Blending Leadership: Six Simple Steps for Leading Online and Off*, Reshan Richards and Stephen Valentine have created a thoughtful and invaluable guide for school administrators in an age of ubiquitous online connectivity. With their impressive understanding of conceptual frameworks and practical realities, Richards and Valentine adeptly convey that successful blended school leaders 'lead the learning and lead by learning' by helping others and learning themselves, and that effective school leaders of online learning do not operate in isolation, but rather are part of a broad, community plan for learning. . . . With *Blending Leadership*, school leaders now have a powerful guide and ally in their community's online and offline developmental journey."

Tom Daccord, director and cofounder of EdTechTeacher

STEPHEN J. VALENTINE
DR. RESHAN RICHARDS

SKETCHNOTES BY BRAD OVENELL-CARTER

BLENDING LEADERSHIP

SIX SIMPLE BELIEFS FOR
LEADING ONLINE AND OFF

DESIGN

MISSION

THOUGHT LEADERSHIP

SHARING

MEETINGS

THE OFF-RAMP

JB JOSSEY-BASS™
A Wiley Brand

Jossey-Bass books and products are available through most bookstores. To contact Jossey-Bass directly call our Customer Care Department within the U.S. at 800–956–7739, outside the U.S. at 317–572–3986, or fax 317–572–4002.

Wiley publishes in a variety of print and electronic formats and by print-on-demand. Some material included with standard print versions of this book may not be included in e-books or in print-on-demand. If this book refers to media such as a CD or DVD that is not included in the version you purchased, you may download this material at http://booksupport.wiley.com. For more information about Wiley products, visit www.wiley.com.

Library of Congress Cataloging-in-Publication Data

Names: Valentine, Stephen J., author. | Richards, Reshan, 1978- author. |
    Ovenell-Carter, Brad, illustrator.
Title: Blending leadership : six simple beliefs for leading online and off /
    Stephen J. Valentine, Dr. Reshan Richards ; sketchnotes by Brad Ovenell-Carter.
Description: San Francisco, CA :Jossey-Bass, 2016. | Includes
    bibliographical references and index.
Identifiers: LCCN 2016006369 | ISBN 9781119222057 (pbk.) |
    ISBN 9781119222156 (ePDF) | ISBN 9781119222224 (epub)
Subjects: LCSH: Educational leadership. | Educational technology.
Classification: LCC LB2806 .V24 2016 | DDC 371.2/011—dc23
    LC record available at http://lccn.loc.gov/2016006369

Cover design: Wiley
Cover illustrations: ©Brad Ovenell-Carter

Printed in the United States of America

FIRST EDITION

PB Printing   10 9 8 7 6 5 4 3 2 1

Steve dedicates this book to Chloe, Hunter, and Amy.
Reshan dedicates this book to his late father-in-law, Robert A. Butler.

CONTENTS

PREFACE

This book started as a 60-minute presentation in which we explored and examined what school leadership looks like in online spaces. After the presentation, we looked at our pile of notes—scrawled on hotel pads and iPad screens—and decided to write down an expanded narrative, adding examples and expressing our beliefs.

At that time, Reshan was beginning his involvement with the Apple Distinguished Educators program, and he had learned the ins and outs of Apple's iBooks Author platform. Given the spontaneous nature of our project, we used that software to publish a first edition of our book. Our goals were to move fast, ship quickly, fix bugs as they appeared, and explore the dynamic possibilities—live Twitter feeds, swipe-ready images, open communication channels between reader and authors—of publishing online.

As we traveled and spoke about the electronic version of the book (everywhere from Boston to Philadelphia to Canada) and interacted with educators from around the country, we realized that the book was changing again.

Our core beliefs became clearer and clearer as people asked us tough questions or assured us that their experiences matched our own. And as we lived with our beliefs, taught with them at both secondary and graduate school levels, led with them, read with them in our heads, and showed up to meetings with them, they functioned as a kind of intellectual flypaper. We would turn to each other or email each other and say, "That was an example of cleaning up spaces" (Belief 2); or we would challenge each other to plan meetings differently rather than using the default mode of calling people together in a room (Belief 4).

We also learned that by shining a light so intensely on leadership in online spaces, we cast a shadow on what leadership looks like in offline spaces. Shift the light and you shift the shadow; shut off the light and you have all shadow. A simple truism emerged: it is both impossible and impractical to articulate a vision about leading online without articulating a vision about leading offline. If you move a leadership practice online, you are making an implicit statement about *all* leadership and followership in your organization, not just *some* leadership and followership in your organization. The same holds true, these days, for keeping leadership practices offline. When, for example, a leader says, "I'm going to cut this meeting short and ask that you all email me your final thoughts," he is implying that the people in the room are responsible enough and professional enough to follow through on an individualized task. He also may be reading the room and being respectful of people's energy and time. Likewise, when a leader shows up in your office to talk to you about something, she is implying that spending time with you is important and that some things are best handled face to face. Talking about leading online and leading offline should not be done in separate conversations. Deficiencies in one or the other reduce your leadership capacity.

Blind spots partially exposed and blinders off, we started writing again. We collected notes and ideas, attaching sticky notes to a printed PDF of the online text. We clipped important articles into our Evernote folder. Our original text—purposefully lean to share the stage with some of the functionalities made possible in a multi-touch book—became larger. And larger. We realized at some point that the iBooks version was like the demo a band makes on their way to figuring out how they really want their songs to sound.

This edition contains some new versions of older songs, some new beliefs (about the maker ethos and storytelling), fresh photos from Unsplash, gleanings from academic journals, ideas from popular researchers, approaches from practitioners, and insights from startup culture. The latter development has been informed by Reshan's recent transition from full-time work in a school to full-time work at his own New York City–based startup, another example of iteration in practice. At the end of each chapter, you will find "Things to Try." Consider these personal challenges to help you exercise your offline, online, and blended leadership muscles. They are guaranteed to alter your perspective and make you aware of opportunities that are just a few steps, or a few keystrokes, away. There are additional sketchnotes from Brad Ovenell-Carter, who has shared the following based on his experiences:

> I love marginalia—those notes and doodles you find left in secondhand books by previous readers. They extend the conversation beyond the author and me, often giving another perspective on how to read the book in hand. Finding marginalia is usually a matter of chance, though I will admit that when choosing two copies of the same book I will leave the cleaner version on the shelf. It is even rarer to find marginalia now that we are moving to digital publications. But now, Steve and Reshan I think may have restored the practice . . . with this wonderful idea of taking those embellishments and baking them into their book as sketch notes.
>
> Sketchnoting is a visual form of note-taking, drawn in real time—in this case, as I read Blending Leadership. That was different. I have been sketchnoting at conferences and presentations for some time, but this is the first time I've drawn notes while reading

a book. Reshan pointed out that reading is a "live" experience so sketchnoting a book shouldn't be all that different. And he was right. I kept to the spirit of that and made my drawings on my first read through the manuscript. So, what you see here are those ideas that resonated for me, recorded as fresh and immediate as though Reshan and Steve were presenting their ideas from the stage.

Back to the story: As our text solidified into its new version, we also realized that, by publishing it exclusively online, we had missed readers who were interested in the concepts we were discussing but couldn't access the book online. Many people still read in a traditional way, turning pages and writing in margins, and we want to connect with these people too.

Why begin a book about school leadership by talking about a pile of notes that became an online text that became the book you are holding? And why admit that so much has changed in our thinking?

Because this is partially a book about how we work in schools and how we *might* work in schools. We are committed to a set of ideas and a process for spreading them. We are trying to capture our evolving understandings and present them. We are trying to reach multiple constituents (in our case, readers) who listen and learn and access information in different ways. Is this not what school leadership is about, too? A constant riffing on a set of core beliefs, rapid prototyping to ensure that we apply what we learn, a continual evolution of program and curriculum—and people—to ensure that our missions play out on modern stages and fields and classrooms, offline and online?

Pulling up the curtain on our own working methods, on the story behind the story, is a critical part of our reflective process, a critical part of what we can share with you, and a critical part of what we hope to model for you. In the online edition and in interviews, we promised to treat each subsequent text like software code—updating it as new ideas presented themselves and the needs of our users (readers) changed. This book, made of paper by design, not default, isolates our core beliefs even more starkly, adds new examples, and generally presents our ideas in a more accessible manner.

That accessibility is important—all-important at this point. Leadership is, after all, almost everyone's job in a school. Whether you are leading the entire school, the board, a department, a committee, a classroom, or a club, you can perform that duty with intention, with a growing number of tools, with a certain attitude, and with a certain mindset.

Our goal is to tell a current—and new—story of school leadership, to model how to make sense of the shifting context in which school leadership happens, and to speculate responsibly about where we think the story of school leadership is headed. This time, our delivery device is a book. Next time? Who knows?

As you read, and react to what you read, please connect with us on Twitter—@reshanrichards, @sjvalentine, @blendingleaders—or Google Plus. We'll be listening.

ACKNOWLEDGMENTS

More than a record of its authors' thoughts, a book is also a record of its authors' affiliations. We have been honored to know, and hope our book honors, the following:

The entire Montclair Kimberley Academy community. MKA is a generous, life-affirming school filled with curious, kind, creative, and supportive people. We defy anyone to join the school—as a teacher, student, or parent—and not be transformed for the better.

Kate Bradford, our editor at Wiley Jossey-Bass. She had faith in this project—and in us—from the start.

Elisha Benjamin, also from Wiley Jossey-Bass, who helped clean up those moments in the text when our exuberance outpaced our syntax.

Brad Ovenell-Carter, illustrator and instigator. He provides a kind of funhouse mirror for our thinking, extending it in delightful and inspiring ways.

Zach Yanes, our research assistant. He was thoughtful, thorough, and even-keeled throughout the writing of this book—exactly what we needed. He has a very bright future, as does any school / company / program with which he is associated.

We also thank everyone who agreed to be interviewed and who contributed ideas to this project. We asked . . . and you answered.

Steve also thanks:

Hunter and Chloe, who cheered for Dad as the pages of this book piled up in the living room and laughed with him when he needed to forget about writing. I write in the morning so you will find me there.

Pearl Rock Kane and the *Klingbrief* editorial team, who push my thinking and inspire me every month.

Michael Brosnan, champion of teacher-writers everywhere, clear thinker, and editor of distinction. He may love the em dash as much as—if not more than—I do.

The Coach and the Gardener (i.e., Jim and Judy Valentine).

Reshan, master learner, masterful teacher, and thoughtful friend. I'll see your five and raise you ten.

And Amy, for whom there are no words except love and gratitude.

Reshan also thanks:

Grayson, Finley, Jennifer, and Riley, who was still unnamed (and unborn!) at the time of manuscript submission, for being a great family of nice people.

The Town School, who took a risk on an inexperienced hire and allowed him to begin his teaching and educational technology career.

The entire Explain Everything team for making the ideas and dreams of many people, including his, come to reality.

Steve, for writing this book. Twice.

ABOUT THE AUTHORS & THE ARTIST

AUTHORS

Stephen J. Valentine is an educator, school leader, writer, and serial collaborator. He serves as the assistant head, Upper School, and director of Academic Leadership at Montclair Kimberley Academy and coordinating editor of *Klingbrief*, a publication of the Klingenstein Center at Columbia University. A frequent contributor to *Independent School* magazine, he also wrote *Everything but Teaching* (2009) and founded Refreshing Wednesday, a company that shapes and ships ideas. He holds degrees from the University of Virginia and Boston College.

Dr. Reshan Richards is an educator, researcher, and entrepreneur. The cofounder and chief learning officer of Explain Everything, Reshan is also adjunct assistant professor at Teachers College, Columbia University. Reshan's scholarly work focuses on the intersection of mobile learning, assessment, and design. An Apple Distinguished Educator and member of Mensa, Reshan has an EdD in Instructional Technology & Media from Teachers College, Columbia University, an EdM in Learning and Teaching from Harvard University and a BA in Music from Columbia University.

ARTIST

Brad Ovenell-Carter is the director of the Centre for Innovation at Mulgrave School in Vancouver, Canada. He never goes anywhere without two sketchbooks and a pencil.

INTRODUCTION

"Leaders 'define reality'" (De Pree, 2004, p. 11). That idea, offered by Max De Pree in *Leadership Is an Art*, is as good a place as any to begin to think about leadership, online and off. It implies both thinking and doing, both strategy and tactics. A leader defining reality must establish the ways in which people interact; the attitudes and approaches an organizational culture will or will not tolerate; the ground rules and guidelines from which activity springs.

THE CASE FOR BLENDED LEADERSHIP

Anyone who works in schools knows that, increasingly, educational activity is shaped and sifted and moderated and facilitated as much online as it is offline. We post resources in online spaces like Canvas or Moodle or Blackboard, and then use those resources to support face-to-face discussions; students email us with questions (and excuses); classroom discussions unfold and are archived for further use in spaces like Edmodo or Schoology; colleagues problem-solve and collaborate in person and then via Google Drive (and Edmodo and email and Blackboard and Moodle and so on). These spaces are all part of our educational reality.

So let's take a step back and think about this new (if you want to call it that) reality. Do you remember the first time you used Google Docs to collaborate? Have you ever taken a moment to study the class webpage where you post your assignments online? Like the food in your mom's proverbial refrigerator, these spaces didn't just appear. Someone outside your school decided to make them happen, and someone inside your school decided to make use of them. Someone made a decision to structure collaboration or instruction or information in a certain way, for a certain reason. The intentionality behind such decisions, we're positing, is a form of leadership.

Under-recognized and increasingly important, this kind of leadership has been quietly evolving and thoughtfully chronicled for at least two decades. Back in 1998, before Reshan or Steve had even entered the educational workforce, Pearl Rock Kane, director of the Klingenstein Center for Independent School Leadership, described leadership-via-network in her influential article, "Farewell, Lone Warrior."

> *Even in corporate America, the John Wayne school of management has given way to an approach that is less hierarchical and more collaborative. In all forms of American organizations there is a desire for participation and teamwork and strong evidence that such participation leads to greater effectiveness. Besides, in a rapidly changing world, even supremely gifted individuals can't handle the amount of work alone or know all they need to know. (Kane, 1998)*

Seventeen years ago, Dr. Kane articulated a vision for leadership—less hierarchical and more collaborative—that would help leaders, both new and seasoned, gain a foothold in increasingly complex schools. Imagine trying to lead a school or department today without collecting multiple viewpoints when facing a problem; imagine trying to lead without delegating or sharing the burden of delivering on your school's mission. The distributed leadership model, described by Dr. Kane, has made school as we know it possible.

And, it can be argued, such distributed leadership began to reach its apex once people in schools were connected by computers and Web servers. Think about how naturally we now join our thoughts via email or a Google Doc or a Padlet wall. Think about the possibilities inherent in designing presentations, or building databases, via shared document workspaces. Think about the data you can examine, and the things you can see in the data you examine, if you have even a rudimentary understanding of Excel.

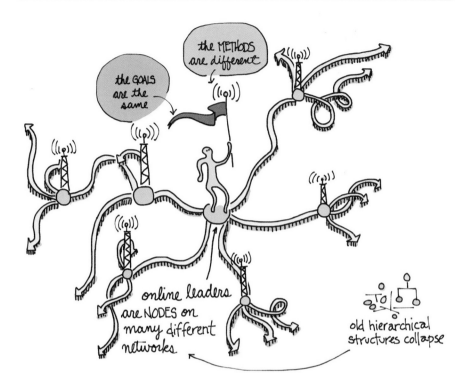

Technology has made possible a new fluidity in leadership thinking, a new fluidity in leadership itself.

Bob Johansen goes a step further in *Leaders Make the Future: Ten New Leadership Skills for an Uncertain World*. In Johansen's lexicon, Kane's nonhierarchical collaborators become transformed, but recognizably so. He urges us to "Think of a leader not just as an individual but as a node on many different networks" (Johansen, 2012, p. 19). The best leaders, accordingly, will be "ravenous networkers with active links all over the world [or, for our purposes, all over the school or schools]."

These quotations tell a story about how leadership has been moving online. But it would be foolish to suggest that online leadership will become the only way to lead in schools. Though folks like Salman Khan have supercharged the possibilities for self-guided study; educational journalists are, almost weekly, proclaiming the death of school as we know it; and LinkedIn has shelled out more than a billion dollars for an online portal (Lynda.com) to help people build skills, most schooling, for better or worse, still unfolds in brick-and-mortar school buildings. Students still attend classes and faculty members still attend faculty meetings. We don't think that you can or should lead schools solely from behind screens.

A recent interview with Henry Mintzberg on the Thinkers 50 website drives home the point, though from a grouchier angle than we'd ever take. Mintzberg accepts the fact that the Internet—via email—has changed the way we manage people, and he's not too happy about the shift:

> [Managers] who rely on email to communicate with their people are in deep trouble. It is a narrow form of communication that's wonderful for getting a lot of data moved around quickly, and for short things (that's why Twitter is its most appropriate form), but it's not the way to communicate fully, richly.
>
> [People] have been managing too superficially. The occupational hazard of managing is superficiality, and these things [that is, email and Twitter] could make it worse. (Mintzberg, 2011)

We concede that any technology, poorly handled, can nullify the personal touch that drives effective communication, teaching, management, and leadership (the list could go on). Indeed, in a 2007 white paper from the Center for Creative Leadership, when asked to choose one skill that is "central to effective virtual leadership," 10 percent of the senior executives surveyed selected "Relationship Building/Face-to-Face Contact" (Criswell & Martin, 2007). Online leadership will never (or probably never) replace the one-on-one, in-person exchange, and we're absolutely not advocating for that. But we want to be clear that, moving forward, the one-on-one, in-person exchange will not be able to replace online leadership either. We don't believe that anyone running a school can suggest that leading online is not a veritable way, that it does not exist, or that it should not persist.

So we've come to a fork in the road, and as Yogi Berra advised, we're going to take it. Should you lead online or should you lead offline? Both. And gracefully, if possible. To lead well today, you have to blend the two approaches. You have to do both well to lead well. Offline leadership and online leadership can complement one another, indeed must complement one another. That complementarity, that blended state, is the story of school leadership today.

Blending your leadership is partially about convenience and scale. The complexity of today's schools was, no doubt, partially caused by technology. And the only way to survive in such schools, the only way to amplify your presence enough to lead in such schools, is to blend online tools into a more traditional leadership approach.

In a day, you couldn't possibly talk to everyone you needed to without emailing or texting some of them. And you couldn't possibly manage all the projects for which you are responsible if you needed to be physically present to connect all the dots.

At the same time, blending your leadership is partially justified by Hersey and Blanchard's concept of situational leadership (1969). According to the model, leaders can lead in one of four ways: by telling, selling, participating, or delegating. Telling or selling occurs when the leader assigns a task to a follower, either directly or via nudges. When participating and delegating, in contrast, leaders develop their colleagues; they help them grow into independent agents or leverage the fact that they are both independent and skilled. Hersey and Blanchard advise leaders to choose a style based on their assessment of the "maturity level" of the colleague with whom they are working. Colleagues who lack skills or confidence need to be assigned tasks; colleagues who demonstrate initiative and skills can receive handoffs and be left alone to carry the ball to the goal line. The jump from situational leadership to blended leadership is, at least on the surface, a small one.

Along Hersey and Blanchard's lines, we might characterize some colleagues as more or less technologically mature than others. Leading them, we have to decide whether we want to work with them in person, via email, or via something more complicated such as nested, shared Google Documents and Folders that require self-direction to access, self-discipline to remember to access, and some skill to operate.

Example #1: One day a senior leader at his school approached Steve about a member of one of his teams. She didn't know this person well and came to Steve's office partially to vent and partially to work toward a solution—she was up against a strict deadline. "I asked him to go online and log into a microsite," she said. "I need him to edit the content. He's the only one who knows [the content] well enough to do so. And he's been unresponsive, at best, and uncooperative, at worst."

Steve knew right away what was going on. The person who was asked to do the editing was very uncomfortable with technology and didn't have a strong enough relationship with the person asking the question to admit that. So he was most certainly avoiding her. If approached directly by her, he would cannily find a way to stall—probably dragging his feet right through and past the deadline.

Steve said, "You've got the right person, but you've assigned him the wrong task. If you want what's in his head, print the website for him and ask him to edit it by hand. You'll get exactly what you need." (Truth be told, the task was poorly constructed and therefore confusing. It's not technically possible to "edit" a website unless you go into the back end. So the leader hadn't blended her leadership very well.) Sure enough, the adjustment of the task—meeting the teacher closer to where he was—made all the difference. He was able to contribute; she hit her deadline; the school profited.

Counterexample #1: On the flipside, one of the complaints that Steve increasingly hears in his role as a school administrator who works closely with teachers is that some leaders are overly reliant on low-tech, or no-tech, approaches. Steve often hears, "We didn't need to do that face to face" or "Why doesn't this team leader use the digital tools available to him through our 1:1 program?" or even, from some design savvy folks, "This leader isn't tending to the user experience very well. If he just took more time to set the task, he would save everyone time and energy." (The last comment is particularly damning; it signals a leader who may be using technology to make his own life easier, rather than the lives of his colleagues.) Some of these "complaining" colleagues would prefer to work in a more distributed manner rather than being asked to convene in rooms according to meeting schedules arranged without their input. Some of them are rising stars in the organization, and they could work in a distributed way and still produce great work. Interestingly, this fact might even reveal the secret to their success. That they are mature in Hersey and Blanchard's sense, and mature in a technological sense, allows them to thrive in the complex, online-again/offline-again kinds of organizations we have today (more on that later).

There are few more overused—although actually useful—lines in education than "meet the students where they are." The same can be said for each of us. Leaders using a blended approach are willing to meet people where they are in order to move their work forward, to move the organization forward, regardless of their feelings about where their colleagues should be on any given spectrum, technological or otherwise. But a blended model of leadership is more than just a convenience—sending effective emails— and more than just a version of situational leadership—knowing when to walk down the hall instead of firing off an email. We can extrapolate from blended learning models to see why, done well and done intentionally, blending technology into leadership practices can add deep and lasting value to a school.

In a book chapter from 2004, Professor Charles R. Graham from Brigham Young University establishes a clear definition of blended learning—one that endures for teaching and learning today and maps easily onto the currently unfolding story of school leadership. According to Graham, the most important component of blended learning is "the combination of instruction from two historically separate models of teaching and learning: traditional F2F [face-to-face] learning systems and distributed learning systems" (Bonk & Graham, 2005, p. 2). He adds that computers are central to blended instruction. According to this definition, school leadership has been blended for years, though for many, in completely unintentional ways. As we move information online, Skype with prospective employees, occasionally replace a faculty meeting with an emailed memo, or pull together a group to participate in a webinar, we are leading in a blended way.

More potent for leaders is the quick Graham statement that follows his definition: "how [learning systems] blend" will be their distinguishing factor. By choosing deliberately the ways in which we engage, or disengage, online tools, we will become effective, even graceful, blended leaders. We will learn to avoid asking each other to complete tasks of which we are not capable, which results in getting frustrated when we can't or won't deliver. Likewise, we will streamline systems using technologies so as to make life easier for each other, to save more of our learning, and to process more quickly those things that can be processed quickly. We believe that leaders need to stand firmly with Graham—how leadership systems blend will be the distinguishing factor for how it feels to work in our schools.

Eliminating frustration in the workplace is important, but that shouldn't be the sole reason to invest in a new method or model. Fortunately, there's more value to be squeezed out of approaching schooling, and the leadership of schooling, in a blended way. Citing the work of several researchers, Graham points out some of the benefits of blended learning, including increases in active learning, peer-to-peer learning, and learner-centered approaches.

No school leader that we know would argue against an approach that will promote active learning, or more peer-to-peer learning, for his or her faculty. In the past five years alone, many teachers, in addition to adding to their content knowledge, have needed to learn (for example) how to use Google Apps, how to use an LMS (learning management system) like Moodle or Blackboard, how to shift to paperless teaching environments, or how to shift from individual paper calendars to shared electronic calendars. If a faculty is not actively learning, and if they are not learning from each other, then that faculty won't grow and progress as it should.

As a leader, if you are responsible for maintaining the quality of a program while ensuring that it advances into the future, you have to ask yourself: Can you afford to lead by "talking at" your faculty, or would you gain more ground by giving your faculty a voice? Can your professional development coordinator teach your faculty everything they need to know, as quickly as they need to know it, or would you be better off if your faculty learned through robust peer-to-peer connections? Can you afford to manage a faculty that is content to slot itself into traditional systems, to fly under the radar, or do you want (need!) a faculty that pushes against systems, that innovates, that co-creates with you and with one another?

Another, simpler way to put it is, do you think of your faculty members as learners? If so, then blended leadership, leadership that carefully and deliberately uses technology to engage and inspire communities of teachers, is worth exploring in more detail. Truth be told, your faculty might even thank you for it.

Horn and Staker published their magisterial *Blended: Using Disruptive Innovation to Improve Schools* in 2014, refining the decade (or more) of blended theory and practice that came before it. In it, they write:

> *Blended learning is not the same as technology-rich instruction. It goes beyond one-to-one computers and high-tech gadgets. Blended learning involves leveraging the Internet to afford each student a more personalized learning experience, meaning increased student control over the time, place, path, and/or pace of his or her learning. (Horn & Staker, 2014, p. 289)*

We don't know of a single adult who wouldn't prefer, as Horn and Staker present it, a blended environment that would give them back some control over their time, the place in which they complete some of their work, and the pace of their work. (Interestingly, this was considered a next frontier in the 2007 Center for Creative Leadership report cited earlier: "Executives See Flex Time as a Concept to Be Taken Seriously" [Criswell & Martin, 2007]). Though we explore work management systems later, looking at the way things like the Agile phenomenon and team management software like Slack might lead to breakthroughs in how we work in schools, even a simple move like allowing a working parent to occasionally phone into an after-school standing meeting—and doing that really, really well—is a huge perk and motivator. Blending technology into daily practice enables you to make such affordances.

As a quick aside, it makes evolutionary sense that thinking about blended leadership would begin to cohere now that blended learning has permeated our schools. After all, our students increasingly come from a "screened-in" environment, cradling iPads while they themselves are still being cradled by parents. Teachers, more and more, come from a similar environment, but there are enough of us who grew up with limited—or no—access to connected screens that covering the range—meeting people where they are, blending when it's going to add deep value—seems to be the best way to lead.

Which leads back to Graham and forward to the central challenge of this book. The challenge is not to add the most technological bells and whistles to your leadership toolbox; nor is it to help teachers add the most bells and whistles to their teaching toolboxes. It is "to try and best understand the strengths and weaknesses of both F2F and CM [computer mediated] environments so that when we are faced with tradeoffs, we can make appropriate decisions" (Bonk & Graham, 2005, p. 17).

Making decisions is indeed crucial, perhaps the most crucial action performed by leaders on a daily, weekly, monthly, and yearly basis.

Regardless of the decision-making process you choose (pros and cons, heuristics, gut level, and so on), weighing tradeoffs is something that all leaders can practice and that will improve. And that will improve their decision-making prowess. The good news is that you don't have to practice on your own school. In an educational climate in which so many practitioners share so much—through blogs and conferences and tweets—and when transparency is such a common value, you can watch others while you are calibrating your own scale of costs and benefits, of trades worth making, hedging, or holding.

LEADERSHIP ANTHROPOLOGY AND LEARNING: LOOKING BACK, LOOKING AROUND, LOOKING FORWARD

In this book we aim to share with you proofs of concept that you can put to use right away. They won't all be easy fits, but if you are willing to tinker with them, willing to take them into your school's proverbial garage and play with them, you will learn a lot in the process and we hope enhance your leadership capacities.

Our examples come from a watchful mode we refer to as leadership anthropology. It's simpler, and ideally less pretentious, than it sounds:

- We look around.
  - What is happening at other schools?
  - What is happening at our own school?
  - What is visible via online networks?
  - What—of what's visible—makes solid sense in terms of leadership practice?

- We think about what has worked in our own working lives.
  - How have we successfully mobilized people around common purposes? How have we organized and completed projects? What has worked, or not worked, for us as followers?
  - How have we learned and what did we do with that learning?

Our approach allows us to write about leadership in a slightly different way than the way others sometimes do. Unlike other leadership books, we try to avoid theories or formulas (though some would argue that the lack of a theory is a theory). Instead, we describe and try to make sense of how people are already leading with technology. This is an important distinction because it recognizes the need to avoid assuming anything about various educational and leadership contexts.

It turns out, the US military, as described in the book *Little Bets*, serves as a useful precursor to this kind of thinking. Peter Sims, cofounder and president of the Silicon Guild, details the shift toward a more context-driven approach:

> *During the Cold War era, the army focused so much on training highly specific, repeatable tasks and eliminating potential errors, that when it faced the new style of insurgent warfare in the Middle East, many soldiers were utterly unprepared. Systems and approved solutions had become too much of a substitute for moment-to-moment, creative problem-solving. To effectively confront the insurgent enemies of today and the future, soldiers must be able to identify and solve unfamiliar problems, rapidly adapting to the circumstances unfolding on the ground. They work from the ground up and must learn from the environment—the people and the situation in each village and town—then craft new tactics that will address the problems they discover. They must be willing and able to adapt to those tactics and keep developing new ones as they go. (Sims, 2011, p. 26)*

A mistake or misinformed effort we often see in the world of educational technology—which is one of the places we often go to find analogies for leadership in this book—is the generalization of problems and "approved solutions" for schools—masking an unwillingness to address the needs of each "village and town," each school. There are so many nuanced layers to what schools can mean, and be, and each layer is dependent on context—locations, demographics, institutional histories, philosophies, and so on. Still, many software providers want to claim to have "the answer" or "something everyone can use." Some even use research from small populations or cases to make broad, sweeping conclusions based on causality that is faulty at best.

Likewise we cannot make the same mistake of prescribing a set of leadership rules that will make someone a better leader. Yes, by reading about and thinking about interesting stories around education, technology, and leadership one can become a more informed leader, but the decision about what is done with that information is what defines "betterness" or "worseness" in any space. Our book shows how successful leaders, online or off, filter and apply those elements that are most valuable and relevant to emergent challenges. Successful leaders reject the idea that leaders have to figure out all the answers—and even ask all the questions—up front. Instead, they learn, and apply their learning, continuously.

That last bit about learning is vitally important and acts as a golden thread for this book. All the examples of blended, and blending, leadership that we found and describe are related in some way to the learning process.

If you think of blended leadership in no other way, think of it this way: Blended leaders lead the learning and lead by learning. Blended leaders alternate seamlessly between those two modes, either helping others learn or learning themselves so as to bring that learning back to the groups they lead. Such practices are sewn into every example in this book.

It doesn't take a brain researcher to know that "learning" has been geo-located to schools and other academic institutions, so much so that some people think that learning can take place only in these places. Additionally, others think that, in order to learn, people have to actively know that they are trying to learn something (for example, by reading this book or searching for articles online).

Our concept of learning is broader than either imposed artificial limitation. Though we are both teachers, we subscribe to the idea (or, rather, fact) that, at its most biological level, learning is the neurological process of the brain evolving (and in some cases devolving) and changing its state to accommodate and then interpret the billions of signals it receives from senses. From this broad perspective, learning starts at gestation and ends only at death. It is not something that starts and stops depending on context. It does not start and stop when one enters or leaves a school. We would not want it, or our leaders, any other way.

Leaders make the learning process transparent and help guide learning toward understood personal and/or shared objectives. Blending leadership just means using some sort of machine-based mediation to drive similar results.

We know from our own experience as leaders and learners that having access to multiple perspectives and being connected to multiple channels of feedback and inspiration, both online and off, provides opportunities for the most informed, empathetic, and efficient response to leadership challenges.

AHMAD'S MAGIC CARD CASE

An email exchange between Reshan and a student (Ahmad) shows the ways in which online interactions can meld with offline interactions and leadership intentions. It would not have happened easily without technology, and the outcome was enhanced by its usage.

Some background: Reshan's desk had been at our middle school campus and Ahmad is a high school student who spends his days on a completely different campus, one mile away. Reshan has never taught Ahmad, and in fact, they do not share a typical student–teacher relationship. Ahmad is a member of our school's laptop leadership team, which means he staffs our tech help desk and is generally charged with helping our 1:1 laptop program to thrive. Reshan coordinates this team, making him a leader of the laptop leaders. He has to help them acquire the necessary skills (or familiarize themselves with the ever-changing world of technology) in order to fulfill their roles appropriately. Like all leaders, Reshan's performance as a leader is only as good as the output of his team.

The exchange begins with the curiosity of the student-leader. Ahmad has a personal interest in our school's 3D printer, and he wants to use it for something fun and test its capacity. "Hello," writes Ahmad; "I want to use the 3D printer at the Middle School and was wondering how I would go about doing so. Could you please get to me on Moodle or e-mail me?"

Upon receiving this email, Reshan has a few choices as a leader. He can (a) call a face-to-face meeting (which, for many leaders, let's admit, is the default mode) or (b) keep the correspondence going via email. He can (c) move through the exchange quickly (to check it off his to-do list) or (d) work through it more slowly so that the student-leader learns more in the process.

Reshan, being a canny blended leader, chooses options b and d. He will keep the conversation online (for reasons that will soon become apparent) and try to enable the maximum conditions for learning. He knows the student-leader is interested and that interest is a powerful component in skill building and knowledge acquisition. He also knows that the more Ahmad learns, the better he will be as a laptop leader. Helping him become as good as he can become in this area will take more time up front, but it will save Reshan time later because Ahmad is a freshman and will most likely be with the program for the next four years. If Ahmad becomes a true computer ace, he will be able to train other students, seek out better resources, offer enhanced technical support to the community, and free up Reshan to do other things.

Without being in the same room with the student, Reshan follows a classic leadership pattern. He offers just enough pressure and just enough support (as leadership guru Michael Fullan [2011] would suggest) to keep Ahmad engaged in the work: "If you . . . create a file (in Tinkercad or Sketchup), then we can print a mini prototype of it for you."

The student then sends along a file, and Reshan responds again, and again chooses to take some extra time (his and the student's) to ensure that maximum development occurs. He decides not to limit the learning inherent in this moment:

> *I could print this for you as is, however I am going to give you a learning challenge. 1) In Self Service -> Applications, download and install Sketchup 2013. 2) Teach yourself how to "close" the spade shapes and then replace it with your initials (either as a cut out or an embossment) or some other interesting thing.*

He then links to a how-to video, which is a key reason to keep the conversation online: permanent resources. If Reshan met with this student and showed him a few moves, the student might not have learned. Or he might have learned enough in the moment to complete the task and then forgotten the steps. Instead, Reshan offers him resources that he can return to again and again. If he encounters a similar problem—say, with a student or teacher he is helping in his role as a laptop leader—he will know how to solve it or know where to look for help.

And so it went . . . until this showed up in Steve's intercampus mail, with a note that said, "Please deliver to Ahmad."

Photo courtesy of the authors

The story of Ahmad's Magic Card Case brings together many threads of blended leadership. First off, it started way before it started, when Reshan and Ahmad built the kind of relationship that could prosper and thrive in either an offline or online space. Then, because of the relationship, they could work together from different campuses for several days in a row—seamlessly. Throughout, the leader-mentor held his protégé in the zone of proximal development, supporting him and pushing him, providing him the resources he needed when he needed them. And the work took place over email, online video, a 3D printer, and finally, intercampus mail.

Without a firm grounding in leadership principles, how they relate to learning, and the work spaces opened up by technology, Reshan never could have proceeded as effectively as a leader. Ahmad's inquiry, and the residual learning it generated, would have gone to waste. Reshan would have bumped into Ahmad every once in a while at an agenda-driven meeting, and the two might not have collaborated. Ahmad might not have added to his skill set.

The potential of what learning can look like today transforms the potential of what leadership can look like today. Ahmad is a student, but he could just as easily have been a colleague. Reshan is a technologist, but he could just as easily have been you, in whatever roles you fill in your school. When the Ahmads of the world approach you, the key habit to develop is to stop time so as to multiply learning. Don't go into instant fixer mode. Ask a simple question instead: "Do you want me to do _____ for you, or do you want to learn how to do it for yourself?" And, if you don't ask that question out loud, ask a version of it to yourself: "If I keep doing _____ for this person, he won't learn. Can I offer him challenge and support instead? Can I commit to his learning instead?"

Maybe the best part of this story is the way it points forward, truly forward. The last time that Steve asked Ahmad for help with something (building a random name-list generator for one of his classes), Ahmad offered his own kind of challenge to Steve, teaching him about Google Add-ons. Of course, Steve wanted Ahmad to just "do it for him," but Ahmad slowed down the exchange, giving more than the answer—he gave Steve a whole new set of tools and the confidence that he can solve at least part of his own problem next time.

WHY WE NEED A CORE SET OF BELIEFS, ESPECIALLY IN THE DIGITAL WORLD

For us, beliefs have become essential lifelines, helping us to lead across platforms and in pockets where many people don't even realize (yet) that intentional leadership is possible. It is possible, for example, to exhibit leadership in the way you, or others, compose email (just take a look at David Sparks's *Email* [2013] from his *MacSparky Field Guide* series if you don't believe us).

It is possible to exhibit leadership by pushing for change in the way your school is represented online via its website or social media accounts. It is possible to lead by collecting and sharing online artifacts.

Our beliefs emerged from many places: from our own practice and observation; from the Ahmads who have entered our lives with curiosity and playfulness, pushing us to turn over our perspectives; from our own leading and teaching; from our own leadership anthropology; from continual conversations with each other and with people at conferences and with authors we have read. As we have tried things or tried them on or looked around or listened or succeeded or failed, belief statements cohered.

And that cohering process has been vitally important—more important, in fact, than the beliefs themselves.

After you have established a set of beliefs about leadership (or teaching and learning, for that matter), other experiences that used to appear random snap into focus. They stick to your beliefs and offer up more meaning. You can understand them, their possibilities, and apprehend them more quickly. Understanding and apprehension lead to meaning—lead to value.

The story of Ahmad's Magic Card Case continues to serve as an example. To explain why he was sending Steve a red card case via intercampus mail, Reshan forwarded him the email string (unpacked earlier) he had developed with Ahmad. It served as a simple request—"Hey, can you give this kid this package"—but Reshan also knew that he was sending Steve a case study, an artifact of a leadership exchange framed by a growth mindset. Steve delivered the package to Ahmad but also appreciated the value. The beliefs in this book helped Steve to see the value implicit in the exchange between Reshan and his protégé and ultimately extract it. Beliefs aid in pattern recognition, which is critical work for a leader, online or off. Beliefs are tiny systems for helping leaders process, chronicle, use, and reuse the digital artifacts and erratum that fly at them. They are tiny systems, too, for maximizing the residual learning effects of aspects of organizational life that many people take for granted: a great email can become a model for other leaders, a school's website can be a model for another school, a collection of tweets can be a breadcrumb trail to the solving of a technical problem.

In their research paper, "Teacher Technology Change: How Knowledge, Beliefs, and Culture Intersect," Peg Ertmer from Purdue University, and Anne Ottenbreit-Leftwich from Indiana University, help us understand how beliefs help us to see, and process, new information.

Tilema (1995) suggested that beliefs act as a lens or filter when processing new information, such as that obtained from textbooks, from knowledgeable others, or even from experience. According to Nespor (1987), early events (especially if particularly unique or vivid) can color our perceptions of subsequent events. Thus new information delivered through professional development programs is filtered through teachers' belief systems before being organized into their existing knowledge structures. (Ertmer & Ottenbreit-Leftwich, 2010, p. 7)

According to this research, investing in professional development without first investing in organizational beliefs is putting the cart before the horse. If teachers don't harbor certain beliefs, they will lack the intellectual flypaper to make learning stick. Activating beliefs is therefore crucial—as crucial, we argue, for leaders as it is for teachers.

LEADERS BUILD BELIEF SYSTEMS

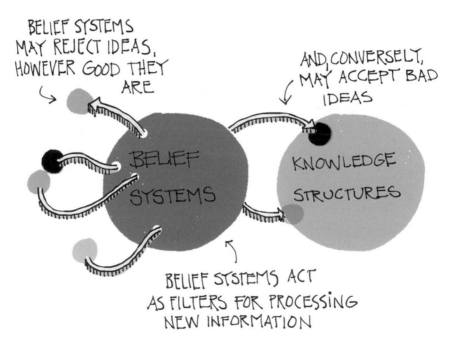

Further evidence suggests that beliefs can ultimately influence behavior, too, making them even more important. In another paper, "Teacher Professionalism and the Emergence of Constructivist-Compatible Pedagogies" by Henry Jay Becker and Margaret M. Riel at the University of California, Irvine (1999), we see that "how teachers organize their classes to a large extent reflects their beliefs about good teaching" (Becker & Riel, 1999,

p. 11). So we act, to some extent, within a range made possible by what we believe, by our beliefs. Also, beliefs influence adult learning and participation in learning communities:

> *Teachers who place a high value on knowledge construction in classroom learning are more likely to play an active role in understanding teaching and learning at their school. Conversely, teachers who focus on delivery of information or skill practices are more likely to spend their free time in the classroom rather than in discussion with teaching peers at their school. (Becker & Riel, 1999, p. 35)*

These granular observations harken back to one of the original, still often quoted leadership thinkers: Peter Drucker. Drucker, in his landmark work *The Effective Executive*, said, "Knowledge is useless to executives unless it has been translated into deeds" (Drucker, 1967, p. xiv). That statement is particularly important in our digital age. Most people are utterly overwhelmed by the digital detritus in their lives—the emails, the websites, the new apps, the app updates, the tweets, the attachments, the Google Docs, the spreadsheets, the infographics, the photos, the likes, the trolls, the spam, the YouTube videos, and so on. They either ignore these artifacts, swat them down, try desperately to combat them with a system, or allow themselves to be washed away in their current. Blended leaders, because of their beliefs, see these objects as fuel for their work. We can update Drucker's words for a new breed of effective executive: digital artifacts and erratum are, in fact, useless unless they have been translated into deeds . . . that is, used as spurs to action, as co-constructive spaces, as models, as test cases, as remixable commodities, as learning opportunities.

Our beliefs for leaders whose work unfolds on and off screens, who blend leadership practices in and out of the digital world, are as follows:

- Belief #1: Blended Leaders engage with thought leaders and engage as thought leaders.
- Belief #2: Blended Leaders design spaces and care for spaces.
- Belief #3: Blended Leaders reject insularity and embrace sharing.
- Belief #4: Blended Leaders challenge meeting structures and change meeting structures.
- Belief #5: Blended Leaders articulate a mission and advance a mission.
- Belief #6: Blended Leaders keep the off-ramp open and use it frequently.

The rest of this book offers a guided tour of each belief—why we developed them, where we have seen them in the world, and how they can help you to blend your leadership so as to lead wisely and well in whatever school context you find yourself.

BELIEFS IN PRACTICE: GETTING READY FOR THINGS TO TRY

 ## An Offline Thing

Make sure you have access to a writing implement, some markers or crayons, paper to write on, sticky notes, and your favorite late afternoon beverage.

 ## An Online Thing

Visit the book's website—http://www.blendingleadership.com—and if you are already active on Twitter and/or Google Plus, find and connect with Steve and Reshan with a follow or an add. If you're not currently active in these spaces, that's okay—you may change your mind as you read this book.

 ## A Blended Thing

Set up blocks of time with digital reminders in your calendar program or on your phone, carving out at least 15–20 minutes of uninterrupted (and uninterruptable) time per week to sit down and engage with this book and the tasks we have designed around it.

Photo by Daniel Bowman

BLENDED LEADERS ENGAGE WITH THOUGHT LEADERS AND ENGAGE AS THOUGHT LEADERS

CROTTY'S WRESTLING

We begin unfolding our beliefs by calling to mind a near-empty school building in the middle of the summer of 2014. A few maintenance professionals are working with light fixtures and air vents; a few more wander through empty hallways slopping paintbrushes into paint. The scheduler processes schedules, the registrar processes grades, and construction on a new building grinds on and then off in a rhythm dictated by a man with a gruff voice. Steve, meanwhile, is fiddling with a pen and pad at his desk, tweaking an agenda for an upcoming leadership retreat. He is stuck—and the building that usually inspires and energizes him, that usually fans his ideas, is failing him. He has no colleagues to bump into, no students to ask him questions, no classroom discussions to shake up his thinking—nothing to break the logjam in his mind.

Steve, like many people in education at that time, had been thinking about grit. He felt it was important for leaders in his school to be aware of the topic, to understand how it might fit into their work with other teachers and with students. He added the topic to his agenda along with a framing question, feeling unsettled about both. Something was missing; he wasn't seeing all the angles; and the books and articles he had read on the subject hadn't helped him to feel settled. Normally when stuck, he would just walk to the office of one of his trusted colleagues . . . or even talk to one of his brightest students. Normally, when school was in full swing, the energy of the place was enough to help him think.

Steve found the support, and the scratch for his itch, on *To Keep Things Whole*, a blog published at regular intervals by Mark Crotty, head of St. John's Episcopal School in Texas. Steve regularly checks in with this blog because Crotty possesses two key characteristics of an effective digital thought leader: a useful, wide-ranging antenna and a quick trigger finger. He picks up important currents in the educational world and then has the discipline and confidence to project his own opinions, his own thinking, into the fray. It was no surprise that Crotty had written about grit at almost the exact moment when Steve was thinking about it.

And it was no surprise that Crotty's thinking was helpful as Steve attempted to plan his team's retreat. The seed of grit—failure—seemed so easy to talk about, but much less easy to accept, much less easy to promote. That was the problem Steve was having with it. Crotty helped Steve make sense of his misgivings when he wrote the following:

> So much of the educational conversation these days focuses on failure and the need for it. Yet one thought keeps nagging at me: Do we really want children to experience failure very often? Part of my concern comes from the word failure. It's a loaded, powerful word, full of psychological barbs. Some argue that we need to soften the word, and that strikes me as a rather quixotic notion. Plus I believe we should keep the word for true failures that deserve it. I keep coming back to Vygotsky's notion of the Zone of Proximal Development, which allows students to work at levels which allow them to experience the right degree of success but also struggle until an adult intercedes at the right moment. It strikes me that's what we want. For students to stumble, trip, fall, then get back up. When this happens while a toddler is learning to walk, we don't call it a failure. I'm not sure why we would with any form of learning. (Crotty, 2013)

Crotty's wrestling with the topic of failure was as good as anything Steve had read about the subject. In fact, it was better because Crotty had seemingly digested the same readings Steve had, and here he was clearing his own thinking, his own reactions, as a thoughtful school leader. Facing a near-empty summertime building, Steve wasn't likely to find a colleague with whom to debate the merits of what he wanted to bring to his retreat. And a phone call to a colleague, most likely at the beach or whiling away the summer with family, didn't seem appropriate. Steve turned to Crotty because, for one, he could access Crotty's thoughts without disturbing him. Also, Crotty had always been a blogger who was willing to embrace, challenge, and frame educational trends.

Reading a blog, in itself, is hardly worth reporting. But reading a blog that you've read before, while carrying in your mind a certain (local) problem you are trying to solve, is a way of working made possible by blending practice. We're emphasizing Steve's interaction with Crotty's blog because it represents a critical habit for school leaders today. They must find ways, and make time, to wade into streams of voices that exist outside the ones they hear in their own, familiar school contexts. These outside voices are valuable in that they exist beyond the constraints established by context (time and place in particular). Steve's time and place couldn't help him; at the same time, his disciplined approach to reading certain blogs, along with knowing how to make use of what he found there, could help him at a crucial time in his summer planning.

There are different names for such practices, which are recognized by researchers as being effective in generating creativity and in aiding effective problem solving. Creativity expert Scott Barry Kaufman, scientific director of the Imagination Institute in the Positive Psychology Center at the University of Pennsylvania, might describe Steve's practice, the one that helped him frame grit and resilience for a leadership team, as an "openness to experience." In his book, *Ungifted: Intelligence Redefined* (2013), Kaufman asserts that openness to experience, in the right amount, is critical to creativity; it can help a person approach a new situation or piece of information without immediately relegating it to a particular category. It also allows us to avoid the immediate conclusion that something is irrelevant. Blogs and other digital scrimshaw are less polished than journals or magazines or books, which frequently employ editors to corral content and proofreaders to reduce language to a single meaning. That doesn't mean blogs are irrelevant or even less relevant, though many people avoid them as sources of knowledge because they want access to knowledge that at least gives off the impression of being "approved." Openness to experience, on the contrary, allows one to learn in places and ways that some people will not.

What becomes critical, then, if you want to take at least some of your cues from blogs, is something that social scientists call "individual absorptive capacity," which, according to researchers Salvatore Parise, Eoin

Whelen, and Steve Todd, is "the ability of employees to identify, assimilate and exploit new ideas" (Parise, Whelen, & Todd, 2015). Paired with openness to experience, it becomes a vital tool for activating knowledge that comes from channels outside the mainstream, or outside the range of voices that you hear on a regular basis. Listening to the same voices creates filter bubbles and redundancy; they tend to reinforce one another's perceptions. Listening to a wide array of voices, some from outside your regular context, and translating them into the community and context in which you work, allows new ideas to enter your closed systems.

Both the givers and the receivers of thought leadership understand that blending leadership can advance their schools. Steve's presentation of grit and resilience, tempered by Crotty's thoughts, achieved its purpose. The leadership team absorbed the trend without becoming fanatical about it; they knew it had some flaws, and they kept this in mind as they worked it into their own daily practices with colleagues and students.

BROADER ENTANGLEMENTS

So some leaders publish and read blogs, and some leaders go a step further, building and sharpening their leadership positions through more active entanglements in the online world. They not only follow thought leaders, but also engage actively with them, building off their work, their thinking, as if it were a platform.

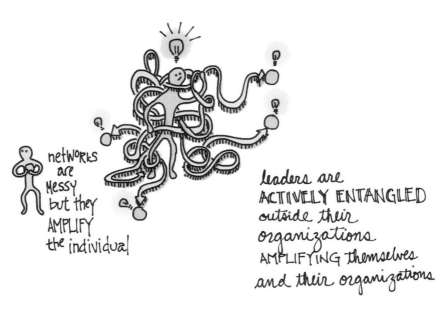

Recently, Reshan followed a tweet by Scott McLeod to a blog post by Larry Cuban. As someone who cares deeply about the place of iPads in education, Reshan was first interested in the conversation because of his respect for the participants. Like Steve, he wanted to see what some of the brightest minds in the field were saying; he wanted to learn from these thinkers and doers.

Clicking the blog, he found that Cuban had used his platform to comment on the Los Angeles Unified School District's deal with Apple. iPads would be distributed to all 650,000 students in the district. Reviewing the deal, Cuban questioned the depth of research that had informed the decision. Additionally, he threw in a dollop of skepticism about the way in which the district had outlined its steps for measuring the success of the initiative as well as the accounting figures.

In the same way that Crotty helped Steve make sense of his own thoughts, Cuban helped Reshan. But as Reshan witnessed the blog's comment tail unfurling, he grew increasingly concerned about some of the oppositions to Cuban's post. He jumped into the fray, extending Cuban's argument:

> *I would suggest that people are looking for or relying on the wrong kind of research, considering how complex educational environments are. I agree with you that the traditional paradigm moves too slowly, so it is up to educational technology researchers to shift the conversation away from the tools themselves and towards learning, pedagogy and assessment. When those things are at the forefront, the constantly evolving technology is much easier to slide into the conversation. Right now it seems that the development and emergence of the tools are driving the learning and pedagogy choices, when it should be the other way around. (Richards, 2013)*

Reshan, as an educational technology researcher and leader, has a stake in any ed tech conversation that garners dozens of comments, as Cuban's blog post did. What's more, his perspective is a valuable one for schools to embrace. Pedagogy should always precede partnerships.

Blended leaders, as depicted in Steve's example, pull in content continually; those same leaders, as depicted in Reshan's example, push back when they need to, just like a leader would push back against a policy in his or her school if that policy seemed poorly reasoned, or worse, antithetical to the relationships educators seek to build with the students in their care. By leveling the proverbial playing field, interconnected computers also extend that playing field. Leaders can "overhear" much more than they used to; they then have to decide whether they want to act on what they hear or ignore it.

Acting helps the thinker with whom you are aligning; at the same time, it leads to co-creative possibilities, enhancing the thinking itself. Reshan's engagement in Cuban's online forum parallels countless other cases in which online collaboration has led to a productive proliferation of information and learning. Rainie and Wellman spend much time in their 2012 book *Networked* profiling individuals from a diverse array of professional and nonprofessional fields who have benefited from the collaborative aspect of online creation. A telling example was the story of Willowaye (a username), a Wikipedia editor. Wikipedia, the ubiquitous online encyclopedia, is well known for being edited and maintained primarily by over 2.8 million non-professional users. During the 2008 presidential campaign, Willowaye found himself in a maelstrom of editors making changes to newly relevant, and oftentimes charged, political pages. Rainie and Wellman observed that

> *the interactions that Willowaye experienced while editing these articles illustrate how networked creators collaborate to produce a collection of valuable information. . . . His editorial experience on Wikipedia during the Obama presidential campaign required that he interact with fellow editors to produce articles about Obama's parents. This often meant that there were back-and-forth discussion of what statements should be included, omitted, enhanced, or downplayed. . . . Creating online material not only gives networked creators a sense of teamwork, but also may lead to new forms of innovation. (Rainie & Wellman, 2012, p. 203)*

Willowaye's creative engagement in an online community (like Reshan's) thus stimulated both his own knowledge and the information available to users through means otherwise impossible to access.

WALKING THE OREGON TRAIL

Before integrated technology was a goal for curricular and instructional leaders, students went to computer class. In the 1980s, students learned Logo or played Math Blaster or perhaps learned to keyboard. Do you remember the original Oregon Trail?

In the 1990s, high school students may have been introduced to hyper-card applications, word processing, spreadsheets, and maybe even some computer programming in languages like C or Java. In the 2000s, computer teachers may have continued teaching keyboarding, while adding the Microsoft Office suite among other software that might be useful in other disciplines. But the computer teacher was the source of the instruction.

In the past decade, the instructional responsibility for computer use has shifted from the computer teacher as a standalone specialist, and his or her class as a "drop-and-go" class, toward a model of integrated educational technology. In this new model, the teaching and application of computer programs is embedded in disciplines or content so that students learn to use the tools in context. The 1:1 computing models, including BYOD (bring your own device) and school-issued devices, have helped eliminate the computer laboratory as a learning space, turning every room into a technology center.

The current situation sounds promising indeed, but in the world of technology, things rarely, if ever, sit still. In the current day, though this concept is being whispered rather than shouted in most quarters, computer science, robotics, design, and engineering together form a discipline that may have more relevance than many other traditional disciplines taught in school. By extension, the question of space has resurfaced. In order to explore these associated ideas, the argument goes, it seems that a return to the computer lab (or design/hacker/makerspace) is necessary.

But what do you do if your school has been spending time and energy integrating technology, only to find that the real truth is this: You need both integrated educational technology (to introduce PowerPoint, Word, and Web research, for example) and computer science (to teach programming, design, and engineering)? Or rather, how do you even find your footing? How do you know which direction is best when, looking back, so much has changed and shifted and, looking forward, so much will change and shift?

If you're a person charged with leading an educational technology program, you might begin by talking to other leaders who are struggling with the same challenges and who are learning from the same experiences. Faced with the queries listed, Reshan attended a monthly meeting of a consortium of regional school technologists who proposed the discussion topic of computer science education. A few people volunteered to share their own approaches, and the coordinator of the consortium (an annual position chosen by the "elders" of the group) was able to bring in someone from CodeAcademy.org to share her perspective. Reshan walked away from the meeting with an understanding: to meaningfully prepare young people to work with technology, schools need to both teach them how to apply tools and applications to different contexts and teach them how to design and program.

More important, for our purposes, is the way in which one can arrive at such certainty, such focus. Today's leaders cannot be insular, gazing at the navels of their own organizations or talking to the same people offering the same predictable advice. Hagel and Brown emphasize and extend this message in a report called "Institutional Innovation."

If we really want to achieve scalable learning, we can't stop at the four walls of the firm. As Bill Joy famously observed, "No matter how many smart people there are within your firm, remember that there are far more smart people outside your firm." We will never learn fast enough if we limit ourselves to the people within any single institution, no matter how large it is and how smart they are. (Hagel & Brown, 2013, p. 9)

Leaders have to be willing to travel outside the "four walls of the firm." They have to follow leadership consultant Les McKeown's advice that a healthy organization will "[expose] itself, through its executives, to other experiences, other realities, other solutions, other questions, other answers" (McKeown, 2010, p. 110). These days, leaders look out for their organizations by looking out of their organizations. Blended leaders, because they break down "time, path, place, and/or pace" specialize in such practice.

IT'S HARD FOR SCHOOL LEADERS
TO GET OUT OF THE BUILDING BUT...

Why? Because blended leaders know that there are many ways to go outside the four walls of their organizations, many ways to examine other realities, solutions, questions, and answers. They know that you don't have to leave school to leave school. Whether they are active professionally on Twitter or Facebook, or spend time reading relevant blogs; whether they engage with others through webinars or the comment functions embedded in various media, blended leaders make it their business to know where to find whatever they happen to be looking for. They are "networked" in the sense described by Rainie and Wellman: "Networked individuals have partial memberships in multiple networks and rely less on permanent membership in settled groups. They must calculate where they can turn for different kinds of help—and what kind of help to offer others as they occupy nodes in others' extended networks" (Rainie & Wellman, 2012, p. 12).

Ronald Burt of the University of Chicago further extends our understanding of the way individuals can span networks to increase their individual performance. In his work *Structural Holes: The Social Structure of Competition*, he outlines two explanations for the inequality of individual performance in the workplace: the Human Capital Theory and the Social Capital Theory:

> *The human capital explanation of the inequality is that the people who do better are more able individuals; they are more intelligent, more attractive, more articulate, more skilled. . . . The social capital metaphor is that the people who do better are somehow better connected. (Burt, 2001, p. 32)*

It is the latter theory in which Burt is interested. In his empirical examination of the social capital metaphor, Burt deals with the inherent gaps in social structure that prohibit relevant information from circulating efficiently between groups. He points out that even if the information being dispersed is of high quality and eventually reaches everyone, this dispersion takes time. This temporal factor means that the person who attains the information earlier has an advantage over the one who learns of it later, and is better equipped to deal with relevant emerging issues. The difference between these two people, Burt argues, is that the person who attained the information earlier was the one who was able to better span the inherent gaps in social structure, or, as Burt calls them, "structural holes."

Burt employs extensive empirical research of American corporations to support his claim that "teams composed of people whose networks extend beyond the team to span structural holes in the company are significantly more likely to be recognized as successful (p. 42)." In a comprehensive employee performance evaluation filled out by managers and coworkers at a large financial organization, Burt found that:

> *Officers with less constrained networks . . . have a significantly higher probability of receiving an outstanding evaluation (-2.3 t-test). The stronger effect is the tendency for officers living in the closeted world of a constrained network to receive a "poor" evaluation (3.3 t-test). (Burt, 2001, p. 41)*

Burt also unearthed a negative association between early promotion, relative salary, bonus compensation, and network constraint among employees. These findings demonstrate the numerous advantages of being a networked individual, unfettered by the "four walls of the firm."

NETWORKING, BUT NOT THAT KIND

In the past, the idea of networking could carry a negative connotation, especially for educators. Some people certainly connect with others online as a form of self-promotion, pushing an agenda that has more to do with their own aspirations for their careers rather than their aspirations for the schools at which they currently work. While this practice is unfortunate—and fairly easy to recognize—it should not tarnish the reputations of those people who are consciously working to build their global, online networks in service of the work they do locally, and offline, at their home base schools.

Indeed, networked individuals bring great potential value to their leadership teams. While they develop personal brands and recognition as their competencies grow, their networking skills allow them to build their support systems (that is, your school's support systems) before they need them. If your school faces a problem the likes of which it has never seen, the most networked individual on your leadership team will know where to turn to begin to address the problem—maybe a blog, maybe a comment stream, maybe a conference or consortium, or maybe another industry altogether. The most networked individual will have a shortlist of people who have demonstrated consistent thoughtfulness, consistent insight, and careful knowledge acquisition over time and outside your school. Though your best solution may come from inside your school, why wouldn't you want to increase your odds of solving a problem by having access to a group of educators and noneducators spanning the globe?

We would go so far as to say that if no one on your leadership team is truly connected to thought leaders, to other leaders, your leadership team is not as strong as it could be. What's more, if you are not actively supporting the ability of someone on your leadership team to function in this way, to get out of the four walls of your school, you are missing a chance to bring a continuous stream of new ideas to the table.

The argument against such drifting—in some senses, against networking in the manner we have put forward—is taken up in a paper by Ray Reagans and Ezra W. Zuckerman. Called "Networks, Diversity, and Productivity: The Social Capital of Corporate R&D Teams," it begins by sketching the lines of a debate between "pessimists, who worry about the coordination problems introduced by demographic diversity [on teams], and optimists, who focus on the learning benefits it provides" (Reagans & Zuckerman, 2001, p. 502).

Citing the work of Pfeffer (1982), Reagans and Zuckerman explain that groups that are "homogenous" are "expected to perform at a higher level because such groups coordinate their actions more easily than diverse teams" (cf. McCain et al., 1983; O'Reilly et al. 1989; Zenger and Lawrence, 1989). This makes sense. If you are working with a team that has similar goals, a common history, role clarity, and a shared sense of the place in which it works, it will efficiently solve problems. It will develop a shorthand that can be especially helpful in a time crunch and trusting relationships that will be especially helpful in a crisis. Its network density—or "average strength of the relationship between team members"—will allow it to establish and implement goals that help the organization as a whole.

Although there are some good reasons to maintain strong homogenous teams, Reagans and Zuckerman demonstrate the benefits of nurturing heterogeneous teams, as well. They cite Burt's theory on structural holes, ultimately presenting heterogeneity as a means to generate learning, ideas, and creativity, and thus drive the performance of teams. Thankfully, and we think wisely, they refuse to solve the debate that they frame at their outset—one between pessimists and optimists—or choose a side, which seems to be the most reasonable and productive way to go for school leaders, as well. They write:

> *A team that does not develop the connections among their members, which enable it to coordinate effectively, faces an uphill battle. However, when such networks remain concentrated among homogeneous sets of individuals, the team fails to generate the learning that can only come from interaction among different individuals. (Reagans & Zuckerman, 2001, pp. 512–513)*

Not resolving the debate with an "either/ . . . or" proclamation presents an opportunity, a justification, for blending your leadership in the ways described in this chapter. Understanding how to lead and participate in a homogeneous group within your school will allow you to generate trust and common purpose and to nurture school traditions that remain worthy and relevant. Understanding how to connect with heterogeneous groups will ensure that your ideas and approaches always remain fresh. Indeed, these practices in some ways are a further articulation of the definition of the blended leader: one who can connect and be effective locally, in person, using the language of the tribe—while also connecting and being effective with more distant circles outside of the time, path, place, and/or pace used by that tribe.

PYRAMID SEARCHING FOR THE GREATER GOOD

How far outside you want to go, and how far is feasible, is a much-scrutinized topic by researchers who study innovation. Marion Poetz (Copenhagen Business School) and Reinhard Prügl (Zeppelin University in Friedrichshafen, Germany) recently touted "pyramid searching" in *Harvard Business Review*, helping us understand how we might use networked intelligence when faced with a unique or challenging problem. The method encourages leaders to network their way to the top of the field of knowledge in which a problem exists. When they reach that peak, according to Poetz and Prügl, they are "more likely to get a referral to someone in a distant but analogous topic area." This allows the pyramid searcher to hop from domain to domain and find innovative, even radical "analogous field solutions" (Poetz & Prügl, 2015, p. 26–27).

Though Steve and Reshan have never consciously practiced pyramid searching, they have felt its impact and seen its results. One of the most beneficial leadership conferences Steve ever attended was an executive coaching conference at which he was the only educator. Everyone else was an executive from a different field. After spending time with a banking executive and a vice president from a family-owned car company, Steve returned to his school and was able to solve one of his knottiest ongoing problems. His colleagues at the conference shook up his typical strategies for dealing with the problem, gave him a new set of questions and tools, and perhaps most important, assured him that he could solve the problem. Back at school, at the level at which the problem was created, people had given up on ever solving the problem. It was considered a sunk cost of the institution.

Reshan also experienced pyramid searching at a conference at which educators and non-educators mixed together to discuss the present state and future of technology. In fact, he uncovered an interesting subset of medical practitioners who had lifted models from education and other industries and applied them to their work.

Ricky Bloomfield, Director of Mobile Technology Strategy and Assistant Professor of Internal Medicine-Pediatrics, told Reshan about interoperability in healthcare:

> Health care is very behind relative to other industries. Just consider how easy it is for you to send money from one bank to the next—even of a competing business!—or for your airline to rebook you on another flight with another airline, if needed. Much has been standardized in other industries, but healthcare is behind. We've looked to those other industries for inspiration regarding how we can make healthcare more interoperable, and to empower patients

by making it easy for them to view and use their own information. (personal communication, August, 2015)

Warren Wiechman, MD, MBA, associate dean for the Division of Instructional Technologies and assistant professor of Clinical Emergency Medicine at UC Irvine Health School of Medicine, continued the themes in Ricky's comments:

In medical education, we're always looking for ways to further engage our students and our faculty with technology. Each poses its unique challenges and oftentimes we try and find solutions amongst other medical education providers. In looking beyond medical education examples, I have had much inspiration for technology engagement and faculty development from K–12 [education].

For our students, the challenge was, how do we get them more engaged with the technology beyond just using it for core functions of note-taking, web-browsing, and email? After attending an Apple event, I saw how K–12 programs (and more specifically K-6 programs) were using their iPads for content creation with video and iBooks; I found this model very easy to adapt into our environment. I also borrowed heavily from "app-smashing" and "app showcases" . . . and adopted them for our medical students.

For our faculty, the issue was professional development—how do you teach them the technology and the ecosystem that comes with it. I got my inspiration here from a K–12 program that leveraged an iTunesU course as a self-directed learning model for basic faculty technology competencies. While the competencies taught are different here on the medical school campus, the concept was the same and we have had good success there.

In both examples, the key was looking outside of the "traditional" environment, finding common challenges, and reworking the solutions into my environment. Having the opportunity to be exposed to these other environments has been absolutely pivotal in making my environment grow and succeed. (personal communication, August, 2015)

Later, as a result of the same conference, Anoop Agrawal, assistant professor at Baylor College of Medicine, spoke enthusiastically about the SAMR model (discussed later in this book):

When you look around medical education, everyone is experimenting randomly without any type of direction or framework. When I stumbled upon SAMR (which I found in Twitter posts from K–12 folks), I was blown away. After [our conference], I saw and heard SAMR spoken of as a core teaching. It has given me a pathway on which to lead the change in medical education, rather than just saying "Look at this iPad! Isn't it awesome?" (personal communication, August, 2015)

Agrawal's enthusiasm led him to share an article with Reshan called "What I Learned about Adverse Events from Captain Sully: It's Not What You Think." Written by Marjorie Podraza Stiegler, MD, Department of Anesthesiology at University of North Carolina at Chapel Hill in 2015, the article acknowledges that some people in the medical community were experiencing "aviation fatigue," tiring of the connections being made between the medical industry and the aviation industry. While model swapping and analogous field solutions might have been drying up between the industries, Stiegler believed that there was more to be gained in relation to our understanding of "second victims," or medical practitioners involved in critical or even fatal events with former patients. After speaking with Captain Chesley "Sully" Sullenberger, made famous by safely landing a damaged plane on the Hudson River, she realized that even if everything seems to go well in a crisis, there could be residual emotional damage for the medical team. She didn't pull a new model from her conversation with Sullenberger, but she did find new questions to ask in her pursuit to provide the best possible care for patients (and the medical practitioners who serve them).

If nothing else, educational leaders should always be on the same kind of lookout, possibly from the height of a pyramid: How can we best care for our students (and the teachers who serve them)?

OUR LEARNING PROCESS MADE VISIBLE

As the previous examples show, we paid a lot of attention to our own learning while writing this book. We included content from things we had read or heard or experienced. That's a given when you're writing a book. You write what you know and learn through your research. The twist for this particular book is that we also thought deeply about how we have learned over the years and how others have led us to learn.

Let us take, for example, some of the guiding leadership principles presented in our introduction. The quotation about leadership from Pearl Rock Kane came to us the old-fashioned way. Steve met Dr. Kane at the Summer Klingenstein Institute, and because he was impressed and enlightened by what she had to say in person, he eventually started reading what Dr. Kane had published. Ultimately, he stumbled upon "Farewell, Lone Warrior," an article whose words have affected his perspective on leadership and learning ever since.

Another one of our guiding leadership definitions came from Robert Johansen. We found this definition, via our own online learning network, by accessing the work of Dr. Michael Ebeling (head of the Summit School in North Carolina). Dr. Ebeling is an example of an effective and insightful sharing leader. If he reads something of value, if he learns something, he seems to share it indiscriminately with whoever happens to be "following" him online. In this case, he advanced our understanding of leadership by tweeting. But there's more to the story. This tweet included a link to an annotation he had made in the book. And the next day, he went a step further by linking to a slideshare presentation on the topic. What's important here is not whether or not we all agree with Johanson via Ebeling. What's important is the way the knowledge came to us—and began to shape our professional lives.

Michael Ebeling @MichaelEbeling   24 Nov
Johansen: "Amplified individuals" in world of connectivity: Best Leaders as "ravenous networkers" amzn.com/k/... Amplified in...
Expand

Part of Dr. Kane's job and calling in life is to mentor emerging leaders. She does this masterfully through her leadership of the Klingenstein Institute. On the surface, Dr. Ebeling's job as head of school is to lead his school. Most likely, he's deeply enmeshed in everything from the hiring of teachers to the raising of money. Most likely, too, he helps leaders in his own school to grow. But he's not responsible for helping two educators in New Jersey (that is, Steve and Reshan) to grow. And yet . . . he has . . . consistently. Michael Ebeling is a leader who is concerned about leadership generally, and he leads others—who knows how many—through the deft use of multiple online platforms. When it comes to Twitter, Kindles, Facebook, iPads and the like, the verdict is still out for many people; while they are making up their minds, blended leaders are trying out the platforms, seeing if they serve a purpose, meeting whoever is already there, and leading within the spaces—because that's what leaders do. They organize around a purpose. They share resources. They develop relationships. They facilitate learning. They get their groups moving.

A PROOF OF CONCEPT

As mentioned at the outset, this book's evolution—from presentation to multi-touch book to the physical book you are currently holding—is proof of the concepts of iteration, versioning, growth, and continuous learning. This book's content is also proof of a certain concept. We started the Beliefs chapter with a belief about thought leaders because much of the book that follows wouldn't have happened without it—without our commitment to learning from those people we could access through our online and offline networks. Sometimes this meant walking down the hall; sometimes it meant traveling to a new city, school, or conference; and sometimes it meant scrolling through a Twitter feed. You can read the rest of the book, in fact, as a narrative driven by network-oriented learning, and as proof of what we found when we blended in with the world (mainly online) while having our feet firmly planted in the world (mainly offline).

We have benefited from being part of homogeneous (in this case, one school) and heterogeneous (in this case, many schools/industries) groups. And, in fact, our membership in both kinds of group has led us into countless scenarios that have either broken down something we thought we knew (helping us to rebuild it) or built up something we thought we knew (helping it to become stronger). It has led, too, to the education that no school could give us . . . because no school has ever been as closely aligned with the actual work we were doing and the actual work we wanted to do.

We don't want to go off on a rant about how you can get all the schooling you need from the Internet. We don't believe that. We believe in the power of interacting, face to face, with caring adults and peers. We believe in developing firm foundations through schooling. We believe that the adults in schools should be each other's best teachers.

But we also believe in a particular kind of leadership intelligence that can be developed and nurtured by interacting with a particular kind of thinker-leader via online networks.

As was written in *The Cluetrain Manifesto*, which has had an enormous influence on modern-day social media, advertising, and communication practices, "networked conversations are enabling powerful new forms of social organization and knowledge exchange to emerge" (Levine, et al., 2001, p. xxiii.). We explore this truism in the remainder of our book.

Another Cluetrain tenet that unlocks powerful learning opportunities for leaders is the confession and assertion that "to traditional corporations, networked conversations may appear confused, may sound confusing. But we are organizing faster than they are. We have better tools, more new ideas, no rules to slow us down" (Levine, 2001, p. xxviii.). Removing the hint of

MICHELLE CORDY ON ATTENTION

If you feed your public quotes and endless links to articles you did not read nor intend to read, they will become quiet ghosts. The power of being online is the abundance of information and people. The possibilities are practically endless for learning and connectivity. This is the great power that all leaders, and all individuals with a Web-enabled device, are able to access. But that power may be undone by a dark and sizable weakness. The great weakness, or potential weakness that leaders must guard against, is managing one's own attention. Howard Rheingold, author of *Net Smart*, argues that we need to develop infotention (Rheingold, 2014), a portmanteau of the words *information, attention*, and *intention*. We must develop a collection of sophisticated tools and couple those with intention, attention, and awareness. Without infotention, we will be led aimlessly through a meaningless forest of Web-linked distractions that will rob us of our capacity for greatness.

—*Michelle Cordy, EdM*

menace from that statement leads us to haystacks in which we might find golden needles. Like authentic learning, blended practice isn't always pretty. As such, many people skip right past opportunities to uncover crucial and relevant lessons.

When you listen and respond to thought leaders, especially the digital kind, communication might look messy or sloppy, maybe even confused or crass, but that's okay. It might unfold in blogs built on free platforms—like Crotty's—or in comments—like Reshan's—logged above or below comments from spammers or trolls. To find Ebeling's tweet on Johansen, you might have had to wade through twenty-five worthless (to you) tweets, fifty worthless tweets, or more. Learning and leading in a blended way means arriving at insights that are not neatly packaged (as if insight could ever arrive that way consistently).

Blended leaders deal with cognitive dissonance and quickly separate digital wheat from chaff. What's more, they don't allow themselves to be put off by chaff. They expect it, have names for it, look past it while toggling between being open to possibility and absorptive to value.

Put another way, blended leaders are the ones with their hands on a radio dial, inching through static in order to find the pure melody that will guide their work. The rest of this book is an example of our tuning and retuning the dial to pick up those distant frequencies, the ones we feel are most important for the future of our schools.

BELIEFS IN PRACTICE: THINGS TO TRY #1

 ### An Offline Thing

Think about the leaders you look up to, whether or not you know them personally. How do you engage with them and how do they engage you? What moves do they make in their own leadership practice that you might try in your own? On a piece of paper, write in one leader's name and then write three words that capture an aspect of his or her leadership style that you admire. Which one is most important or relevant to you? Circle it. Is one dependent on another? Draw arrows to reflect those relationships. Fold (if necessary) this piece of paper and insert it after the last page of this book where it meets the back cover.

 ### An Online Thing

Find an online resource (article, blog post, website, and so on) that was shared with you recently and that you found interesting. Leave a constructive response and/or comment for the author describing a point that you liked or disliked, or with which you agreed or disagreed. Check back in a few days to see if the author responded to your comment. If you want a safe space to practice this move, go to either of our blogs (www.refreshingwednesday.com or www.constructivisttoolkit.com) and respond to one of our posts.

 ### A Blended Thing

Think about something face to face that is coming up next week (for example, a lesson, a meeting agenda item, an assembly topic). Go to http://www.twitter. com (or if you are a current Twitter user, to your preferred Twitter app/ access point) and search for that thing. Spend a few minutes scrolling and clicking through the search results. When you find one (or two or three) relevant and helpful items, favorite (or copy/paste them), and make a point of mentioning or sharing the item next week with the appropriate audience.

Photo by Robin Berghuijs

—————————— BELIEF #2 ——————————

BLENDED LEADERS DESIGN SPACES AND CARE FOR SPACES

IKEA BOXES AND GARBAGE CANS

Recently, during the month of May, Reshan ran an entrepreneurial class for high school seniors. Called Startup 101, the class served as an internship-type opportunity because the students had completed the rest of their high school course work. He—and they—had a great deal of autonomy, and based on what Steve had heard about Reshan's plans, he was looking forward to spending time in the room, watching the experience unfold.

Prior to opening day, Reshan and Steve went to IKEA to get furniture, lighting, and a few other items to ensure that the basement science lab allotted for the course could be converted appropriately for a different kind of work experience. At the end of their shopping trip, Reshan and Steve dropped off a small pile of IKEA loot, efficiently packed in the company's trademark flat boxes.

On launch day, a Monday, Steve eagerly walked down to the classroom. Reshan had promised not only an interesting experience, but also a transformed space. His plan was to assemble the furniture on the preceding Friday. Steve arrived, camera in hand, ready to both experience and document a new space—ready to be transported to a startup-style office that had, only days before, been a working science lab.

But the space was unchanged. It was still the same old science lab—with a sad-looking beanbag chair draped over one of the benches.

Reshan explained that his plans on Friday had been interrupted. Constrained by time, he made a snap decision to leave the IKEA goods boxed and to figure out what to do on Monday. So here's what happened.

When the students arrived on Monday, they looked around at the assortment of chairs, couches, and boxes, and most of them seemed confused. Like Steve, they too had walked in with certain assumptions, certain mental pictures of what to expect. What's more, they had walked in with a standard high school hierarchy in mind: The teacher makes most of the decisions. But then, one student looked at the boxes and said, "Oh—are we going to get to build the furniture? Awesome!"

Photo courtesy of the authors

In that moment, Reshan made a design decision. Instead of directing the students about how to set up the room, and instead of dismissing them for a few hours and setting up the room himself, he dismissed himself. He dropped the default—that the teacher sets up the classroom space—and left for two and half hours after asking the students to set up the room in a way they thought would best serve their work and their aspirations over the next month.

When he returned, the room was completely transformed. Not what he expected, but better.

Photo courtesy of the authors

The students had created a symmetrical conference table, a comfortable sitting area, and an area for food and snacks. When Reshan asked them what else they needed or wanted to bring, they gave him a short list— including a video game console that they planned to run through the overhead projector. He continued his radical design experiment and said yes to anything—within reason—that they thought could support them in their work (and their needed rest from that work). They would, after all, be in the room for very long stretches of time.

The thing that impressed Reshan the most was that all the garbage and boxes had been taken out into the hallway bins. The students clearly "owned" the space and wanted to take care of it. What's more, the first day was supposed to wrap up at 2:00 p.m., but most of the students remained in the room until well after 3:00, talking and working. On day 2, students had a choice about showing up in person or working from home on a task list established during day 1; all of them showed up, save for the students who had other school responsibilities; they wanted to work in "their space." Reshan's quick design decision transformed a space; also, it transformed the motivation of the students assigned to work there (we catch up with this group later on and see what they were able to build).

Working with spaces in schools is not always so inspirational. One of the most memorable acts of school leadership Steve ever engaged in took place at the Johns Hopkins Center for Talented Youth. After teaching in the program for several summers, he had become an academic dean. When he arrived at the site that summer, head filled with visions for curricular and pedagogical innovation, the site director handed him a clipboard and told him to make sure all the classrooms had garbage cans.

What? Was this really something on which an educational leader should be spending his time? In this case, yes. Steve was responding to feedback from past groups of instructors and taking care of the basic needs of the current ones. If they showed up and saw garbage cans in their classrooms, they would realize that Steve and his team were tending to their needs. A small act, delegated from the site director to his academic dean, set the tone for positive relationships between the administration and the faculty, and by extension, between the faculty and the students.

More than just setting a tone, though, the placement and existence of the garbage cans enabled teachers to do the work they had signed up to do—teach gifted and talented students at the highest possible level—rather than having them worry about where they were going to deposit the trash that accumulated when a single class stayed in a single classroom for six hours straight, five days a week.

So what do IKEA boxes and garbage cans have to do with blended leadership? What do these physical spaces have to do with the kinds of online/offline spaces that many of us encounter in our daily work?

Spend time in school and you spend time in spaces. Pencil cases and lunch boxes in the early days. Lockers and backpacks later. Classrooms, dining halls, lounges, offices, performance centers, labs, and gymnasiums throughout. And, increasingly, whether you are a student, teacher, or school leader, you also spend time in online spaces. You don't walk into them (yet). You enter them after clicking a few keys or putting on headphones or tapping your phone. You enter them when a colleague tells you to click on a link that encourages you click on another link, and another. You enter them when you set up a course management system.

And leaders—the blended sort we have been talking about in this book—take full responsibility for online spaces, as they take full responsibility for offline spaces. Blended leaders recognize that spaces, offline and on, can be designed (well, passably, or poorly) and cared for (well, passably, or poorly) and that the elegant blending of offline and online space is possible, and maybe even preferable, in the schools we have today.

Approaching spaces with a design eye means avoiding the default—the worn grooves of leadership and practice. It means thinking about the designated user, the problem that user is trying to solve, and in some cases, allowing that user to make choices about how the space will relate to, and support, the work that unfolds in it. It's a simple, though radical shift. After all, when was the last time you started a class or meeting by asking for input on the use of the space? When was the last time you included in a survey of your class a question about the layout of your course management system? Are you willing to teach or lead from a new place or in a new place in an old space?

Approaching spaces with an eye toward maintenance, toward care, means ensuring that the space remains maximally usable—that nothing gets in the way of the core purpose of the space. It means caring for the space in a way that everyone feels compelled to continue to use it, or even better, to care for it themselves. Caring for space offline is instantly recognizable. You roll up your sleeves to rearrange furniture. You clean up after a dance or party. You replace a bulb or add a recycling bin. Of course, caring for spaces is also possible in the online world, even though such leadership is largely invisible. For example, when an administrator or teacher fires up a computer, if everything works as it should, she is the beneficiary of such leadership. She sends the emails she needs to send or updates her calendar or posts an assignment or designs an activity. The ease with which she works is directly proportional to the quality of decisions that were made behind the scenes about the online platforms that drive and enable much of her educational work. What options and limits should she have? What bells and whistles? Should her online gradebook have built-in values for grades? Should her course management system contain templates or remain relatively flexible? Should her faculty email contain a standard sign-off?

In an effort to design and then care for digital spaces, leaders, both offline and online, grapple continuously with the questions in the previous two paragraphs along with a slew of others. Such grappling matters because it is a sign of good faith and, done well, it leads to one of the most important ingredients in successful collaboration between leaders and followers: trust.

In Reshan's first formal school role, he was a member of a technology department that provided technical and technology-related instructional support to faculty and staff. Completely new to the world of teaching and learning, Reshan mostly handled technology support requests like fixing printers, repairing network connections, and installing software. During his first three years in this role, three mechanisms were developed by the department to field technology requests: a generic email address that forwarded to all members of the department; a Web-based form that, when complete, would send an email with the results to the previously mentioned generic email address (helpful when a person is having trouble with his or her email); and a phone/voicemail extension that, when messages were left, made an indicator light appear on the desk phones of the four department members (helpful when the person is having trouble with his or her email and accessing the Internet).

The human challenge of such an online system was that people were used to contacting an individual directly, not a shared space or service. Subsequently, all the department members found that they were not only trying to manage the requests coming through the designed mechanisms, but also trying to respond to requests coming through their individual emails, individual voicemails, and perhaps most frequently, their face-to-face interactions with people. It became a hard sell, when speaking with someone in person about a problem he was having, to tell him to go back to his classroom, make a phone call to a generic voicemail, and leave a detailed message. Adding to the perceived absurdity, there was a 25 percent chance (or more, depending on how busy the department was) that the person standing in front of him would field the request anyway.

So the blended solution was as follows: the generic mechanisms (email, Web form, voicemail) would remain and the faculty and staff would be encouraged, but not required, to use them. Then, the technology department members would log any and all requests in an asynchronous, collaborative spreadsheet created on a networked drive. For face-to-face conversations, passing hallway mentions, and office drop-ins, technology department members would try to log the request immediately in the spreadsheet (if there was access), jot it down on a piece of paper (if there was one available), or politely ask the person to send it to the individual tech department member (not the generic line) via email or voicemail.

Such a solution certainly created more busy work for the technology department members. But it also helped to promote in the school a culture of trust that the department was supportive, flexible, and responsive. Over the years, more people began to trust and use the generic system because of faith in the people behind the system.

SOMETHING EVERYONE CAN USE

Designing spaces could involve developing complicated architectural plans, writing HTML code, or creating an asynchronous, collaborative spreadsheet. . . . It could involve knocking down walls or painting white boards onto existing walls. But it can also start on a much smaller scale. It can start with something as accessible, user friendly, and widespread as Google Docs, a tool of choice for many school leaders.

Reshan and Steve often ask members of their departments or committees to contribute to shared Google Documents or to respond to Google Forms. And, though the tools will change over time, these instruments offer an instructive, emblematic place to begin our consideration of digital space. Because, when you plan to use a Google Doc, designing the space to collect thoughts is the first step. You will want to make sure that you think through what you are hoping to collect in the space, and how best to organize the buckets into which information will flow. The space should have adequate headers and embedded questions so that contributors know where to add their thoughts. Clear directions at the top help as well. We're pointing out what may be obvious to some in order to highlight the kind of "design pause" that is necessary to shape space for users. Rushing people into a space can leave them disoriented or disengaged, and leave you feeling unsatisfied with their performance. Taking a few minutes to prepare for their arrival—as you would in your office or home—can make a big difference.

But you certainly shouldn't stop there. Once people start to contribute to the document, you have to care for the space, refining and revising the document. If you have used Google Docs with a group of people, you know that shared documents can quickly fill up with multiple colored and sized fonts, a variety of sentence and paragraph structures, and thoughts that are half-formed, redundant, or overly wordy. The leader's job, in the case of Google Docs, is to edit, reshuffle, cut, and where necessary, ask clarifying questions so that the document remains eminently usable for everyone.

BOOKS BY GUYS NAMED DAVID

MESSY SPACES LOWER THE SIGNAL: NOISE RATIO AND MORE NOISE WEAKENS THE MESSAGE.

WEAK MESSAGES CREATE BAD SITUATIONS

SHRIGLEY

HOW MUSIC WORKS

BYRNE

ENVIRONMENT DETERMINES CONTENT. SO, MESSY SPACES MAKE MESSY CONTENT

ALSO, TWO OF THE BEST BOOKS ABOUT EDUCATION THAT AREN'T ABOUT EDUCATION.

The writing of this book is a good case to highlight. Steve and Reshan drafted the text for this book in a Google Doc. When it started, the document not only contained the book chapter drafts, but also it held an outline, links, inspirational notes, and a lot of other items related to the completely online collaborative process to which we agreed at the outset. Once the writing of chapters started to take off, with Steve and Reshan dropping in ideas, images, quotes, phrases, and various marginalia using the Comment function, the document was a mess we both had to scroll through each time we wanted to add something.

Reshan decided to create a second Google Doc and moved from the first document anything that wasn't a direct part of the text. He moved references, writing ideas, and marketing ideas; then he went a step further. In the main document he created chapters and bookmarks, and used page breaks and horizontal rules to organize the information.

Though Steve couldn't observe the work, though he couldn't see the effort, he benefited from it right away. Reshan took a break from writing—a design pause—to care for the space in which we were writing. Did this help the writing? In the short run, no. It didn't help to add raw word count to the text. And it knocked us off schedule a little bit. But, in the long run, it absolutely helped.

Reducing clutter allowed us to think clearly and to quickly arrive, with one simple click, at the part of the book on which we wanted to work. For Steve, this redesign of his digital workspace felt like walking into his house and finding that someone had organized it, cleaned it, and thrown away unnecessary items. The experience refreshed and energized him as he approached his responsibilities in writing certain chapters.

The Google Doc tool itself serves as a wonderful spur to collaboration, but it has limits. The tool cannot design itself at the outset, and it cannot reorganize or declutter itself so that the best, most workable ideas rise to the surface. The tool cannot reach out to its users and adjust itself based on their preferences (at least not yet). The tool cannot synthesize or make meaning. As they would in the offline world, these tasks fall to the leader: the human, not the machine.

Our own work in Google Docs drives the advice we give others when consulted. For example, we recently worked with someone who was in charge of unifying departments across three campuses and looking to serve her community by helping to address the typical school problem of vertical curricular alignment. She wanted to ensure that all members of each department had a voice. She reached out to us because she saw it as a blended leadership issue that would require a technological fix, and she wanted to use her school's ample and enviable technological resources. After offering her a technological solution, though, we quickly added an addendum about the necessity of ongoing maintenance, of caring for the space. None of our suggestions would matter or stick if a dedicated leader didn't take responsibility for the project—if a leader didn't adjust his or her work priorities to truly care for, and develop, the space. We wrote her an email, which we have copied here, because it is easily generalizable to many situations where we need to seek balance between technological and human elements:

One of the major challenges to first think about is how to keep whatever system you develop afloat. You can build almost anything, but if you don't find ways to entice people to use it and keep going back to it, it will almost certainly fall flat.

The leader has to be very committed, outside of the regularly structured meetings, to pull in content, edit it, format it, send reminders and updates, etc.

Perhaps you can start with a highly curated shared Google Doc, one that includes a simple, though strong, header structure for the different campuses. There could be a period of posting, followed by a period of commenting. This can help members of the department develop a simple rhythm.

Another option may be to generate an initial group of comments: a leader could ask the group to respond (via email) to a prompt. He/she could then publish the responses via a Google+ community or a Google Doc or a blog that is open to comments (or even a follow up email).

The driving initial question is: is there a person in the school who has the time, energy, and talent to prompt the writers (teachers), to clean up and post the prompts, and then to prompt people for comments? The choice of platform doesn't matter as much as the force behind the conversation. No driving force = certain failure. (Richards, personal communication, November, 2013)

A sloppy Google Doc that is not well cared for sends a poor message. Technological spaces that are wound up and left to run without care will soon be digital ghost towns. In our experience, one of the easiest things to do is to send around a Google Doc. One of the hardest things to do is to keep it clean and fluid—a space that serves its collaborators.

We have all had the experience of receiving targeted ads (say, while composing email in Gmail or Yahoo) that have absolutely nothing to do with our interests or activities. When this happens, when mere noise is presented as a gift, we feel that we are interacting with a technological algorithm, one that thinks it knows us, rather than a human being, one that can be appropriately intentional when seeking our attention. Noise is not good for the company providing it or the person breaking his or her concentration to process it.

If you want the people you lead to be the beneficiaries of technology and feel comfortable entering technological spaces to perform job tasks more efficiently and even joyfully, they must feel that an interested, empathetic leader is monitoring those spaces and making continual adjustments to improve them. To care for digital spaces, you have to care enough to push into them and continually sand them down, like a digital Zamboni driver who arrives, systematically and predictably, between the action on the ice.

Such work takes time—the kind of time that leaders, frankly, do not have for themselves and often do not grant to others. When you're working online, no one offline can see you sweat. You're just pecking away on a laptop. You're trading presence offline (say, in roaming the halls or visiting classes) for presence online (say, in connecting documents or altering where things are stored). Offline leaders reared in certain leadership contexts swoop charismatically into rooms. Online leaders serving young adults who grew up gaming and older adults who grew up before cell phones sometimes have to tiptoe out of those rooms in order to adjust comment settings or margins or headers or invite lists or permissions.

But make no mistake: Performing the kinds of work described in this chapter is a twenty-first-century version of servant leadership. Robert Greenleaf, who coined the term, tested servant leadership behavior by asking if it made others "freer, more autonomous" (Greenleaf, 1977, p. 281); the person making sure that digital spaces help teachers to collaborate better, problem-solve better, create better, is a thoroughly modern servant leader.

A PLATFORM FOR PROFESSIONAL GROWTH

Indeed, online spaces properly constructed and maintained can help the servant leader model scale in schools. You can serve one person—making him or her more autonomous—by designing a great document. You can serve many people—making them more autonomous—by developing a platform to support and enrich their work, and making sure the platform changes as their needs change.

Almost five years ago, a committee on which Steve was a key member revamped entirely his school's Professional Growth Program (PGP). They rewrote the mission of the program, all associated protocols, and all guiding documents. To house this new program, the leaders of the PGP Committee decided that they needed to find a way to store and present information, to allow people to interact with that information, and to create a space for shared reflections as well as forums. Steve and his colleagues knew that the tying together of all these functions and documents could best happen in an online environment. They had several meetings where they drew mock-ups, reviewed Web applications, and bemoaned the fact that the perfect online environment didn't seem to exist. Had they the money and the time, they would have tried to invent something themselves.

At one point, a committee member discovered Ning, and the first chapter of the PGP really began to take shape. Ning allowed individuals or businesses to set up standalone, customizable social networks, leveraging Facebook-like connectivity and shareability while keeping people within a "walled garden." The ISEd Ning (short for Independent School Educators network) was developed as a social network playground and experimental space for educators to explore, share, and discuss topics of interest, videos, podcasts, blog posts and more. This community of well over five thousand members continued to be an active forum for a number of years. (*Note*: Ning transitioned from being a "free-mium" service to a completely paid service, but it allowed any existing Ning communities to continue to operate for free.)

The first iteration of the online space to support the school's professional development and evaluation cycle was set up as a subpage of the ISEd Ning. Considering the robust presence of educators already involved with ISEd, Steve and his colleagues, Jenny Zagariello and Karen Newman, believed that ISEd would be a great place to house their school's resources for the PGP. The intent of the PGP subpage was not only for the school to create a repository for all its professional development resources; the design of the online space also facilitated the type of growth-oriented participation that the educational leaders at this school were looking to leverage.

Unlike Steve in the garbage can example at the start of the chapter, an online leader cannot expect to simply set up a space and move on; the ongoing care for digital spaces extends their effectiveness and promotes engagement by all constituents and users. So, in the case of the Professional Growth Group on the Ning, Jenny took the lead in caring for the space. She updated resources based on feedback. She created an index with categories so that resources appeared in a more organized manner. She helped people who had trouble logging in or who were inadvertently kicked off the Ning by glitches in the system. She communicated directly with Demetri Orlando, who was in charge of the ISEd Ning, whenever there was a problem or in advance of sending the entire faculty to the site, to ensure that the concurrent hits wouldn't somehow crash it. In short, her online leadership, behind the scenes, ensured that the school faculty was supported as much as possible during their transition to a new and complex professional growth program and its platform.

At the end of the first three-year cycle of the PGP, the PGP Committee collected feedback about everything from the growth protocols to the rubric driving the growth protocols to the use of ISEd as a backbone for the entire project. The community was loudest and clearest in regards to their desire for a simplified and streamlined process. The Ning was certainly part of the solution, but it was also part of the problem. Though well intentioned and well managed on our end, it lacked a few key usability factors.

People critiqued the site itself, and the tools it offered. They noted simple things like the problem of having to remember another username and password or having trouble with their usernames and passwords. They had difficulty finding their way around the Ning or establishing a workflow. They found that the site contained too many links, too many things to click on, and not enough guidance.

Now, frankly, some offline leaders would laugh at you if you told them you were thinking about your colleagues' behaviors in such minuscule ways. You wouldn't have to tell a group of teachers how to use a door to enter a classroom or how to walk around that classroom. And you shouldn't have to help professionals remember usernames and passwords. That's true on some levels, but in the online world, the design interface is of critical importance, and effective online leaders pay particular attention to the way design affects behavior. Nabeel Ahmad, a Learning Developer at the IBM Center for Advanced Learning, has stated that the more menu clicks in a web or mobile environment, "the higher the likelihood of distraction," and the higher the likelihood that "the user will deviate from the original intent" (Ahmad & Orton, 2010). As such, an effective online leader will work to reduce the clicks it takes for the end user to complete a task. Dan Saffer, a designer and author, adds this real world example: "Why do Windows and Mac OS X, which basically do the same thing and can, with some tinkering, even look identical, feel so different? It's because interaction design is about behavior, and behavior is much harder to observe and understand than appearance. It's much easier to notice and discuss a garish color than a subtle transaction that may, over time, drive you crazy" (Saffer, 2007, pp. 3–4).

If an online environment does not work smoothly, if it appears to be broken, if people leave the site to dig up a password stored in their email, their workflow for that particular task might be irreparably broken. They certainly will not be able to focus on something as complex as their own professional growth.

Other changes signaled the end of the Ning for this school. Jenny, who best understood the Ning, had moved into consulting work. Ning itself was going through an identity crisis trying to figure out its business model. The committee was not sure that Ning would even exist in a usable form for the school's purposes in a few more years. As is discussed again later in this book, blended leaders always have to try to guess the next iteration of a product . . . and be ready for its demise.

DON BUCKLEY ON DESIGN

Everything around us is designed, but we usually associate the term *design* with products. However, more and more in the twenty-first century we have started to accept that systems, experiences, and services are also designed. So leadership is, can be, and needs to be both designed and intentional. Design thinking needs to be part of our everyday habits because we live in world of complex and ambiguous problems.

—Don Buckley, cofounder, Tools at Schools

All these factors contributed to one of Reshan's and Steve's first collaborative projects: the redesign of the PGP site. With the guidance of the PGP Committee, we decided to abandon the Ning and build our own website. Simplicity and usability were our primary goals. We decluttered the site, made people's usernames and passwords the same as they are to log into school email, and asked Alicia Cuccolo, a talented artist and art teacher at the school, to design a logo that would encapsulate the driving spirit of the program. When we explained the new PGP (called PGP 2.0 to signify a second iteration and to remind people that, in the world we live in, flux is the only constant), the loudest applause was reserved for the new online interface. Rather than having to find their way around the Ning, people could focus on their growth and development.

MONITORING SUCCESSFUL VENTURES

When Reshan started as director of educational technology, he inherited oversight of Moodle, his school's course management system. Moodle had been set up in such a way that there was an incredible amount of teacher use of this space as an extension of the classroom; additionally, committees and leadership teams used the space to organize their work. All the school's professional development resources were posted there.

Over time, however, Moodle became a victim of its own success. Remnants from previous years began to add up. People were starting to complain about the long lists of courses they had to scroll through to find their current courses. Students and teachers had no idea how to find certain things. There were links and resources that dated back several years. The color scheme was an unpleasant, to say the least, beige and brown. The faculty's high usage of Moodle led to Moodle being difficult for faculty to use.

The people in charge of managing Moodle had a good problem; the teachers and the greater school's understanding of online spaces as part of the learning environment created a burgeoning shared space in need of some serious curating. Reshan set aside several weeks of his summer to completely overhaul the internal and external structures without compromising existing materials or the shared understanding (among administrators, faculty, and students) of how the environment functioned.

The redesign of Moodle had two major purposes. First, some clean-up needed to be done to make the experience of using it more palatable. Second, the redesign was a simple act of practicing what one preaches—of modeling. Teachers are asked to maintain and curate these online learning spaces for students (their primary constituent); the one with the power to make the design environment as usable and friendly as possible for teachers has a responsibility to do so also.

Course management system administrators should systematically check in with teachers to ensure their online experience is smooth; the hope is that the teachers will then systematically check in with their students. Good practice is a virtuous cycle.

MANAGING BY SURFING AROUND

The example presented is about a leader being receptive to what he learns by watching, and listening to, users in a space over time. By making adjustments—some of which people knew they wanted and some of which they didn't even know were possible—Reshan modeled the need to be as responsive to a virtual burst pipe online as he would be to an actual burst pipe offline. Digital wall rot has real consequences over time.

A leader need not stop there, however; it's also possible to drive change in an online space; to not only learn about the needs of users, but also to manage or lead those users by making your presence known, by actively collaboratively to solve problems, by spreading your own beliefs about optimal behaviors—by entering the space in order to maintain or promote excellence in it. We call this practice Management By Surfing Around (MBSA), a derivative of Management By Wandering Around (MBWA).

MBWA was practiced by David Packard of Hewlett-Packard, popularized by the bullhorn of Tom Peters, and continues to startle leaders and followers who sometimes forget that they can diverge from the kind of prearranged partnerships that occasionally (or more than occasionally) make the workaday world so stale. MBWA's ascendancy and core principles continue to be well documented. Recently, for example, Peter Sims wrote in *Little Bets*, "Gathering insights from people doing the work seems like such an obvious (and fairly common) way to be a better-informed leader and person, but in the early 1980s, it wasn't a mainstream management practice" (Sims, 2011, pp. 120–21).

The classroom visit/observation/evaluation lands in the job description of many school leaders. They walk into classrooms, either scheduled or unscheduled, as a way to understand what is happening in their schools. These visits help them to be more informed, and done well, become a powerful tool for both supervision and growth. The last time Steve was observed, he ended up working with the observer to fix a very simple issue: the physical spot where he taught in the classroom. At times, the place where he settled moved some students into his blind spot. After receiving the feedback, and knowing that habits are difficult to break, Steve started randomizing the seating in most of the classes that followed. This ensured that students were always in different parts of the room and would receive equal amounts of his attention. By using a school leader's version of MBWA, a school leader helped Steve to better help his students.

But Steve does not just teach in the classroom anymore. He teaches in Moodle and Edmodo and Google Docs. He facilitates discussions in these places, posts resources in these places, and asks questions in these places— sometimes from the comfort of his own home. To become a complete teacher, and to continue to grow, he needs feedback in the online realm of his teaching—the design choices he makes, the quality and warmth of his communication, and the freshness of his content, to name but a few categories. And to become a complete leader, he needs to click around on the Moodle pages of the teachers at his school, he needs to "drop in" to the online extensions to their brick-and-mortar classrooms. He needs to incorporate Management by Surfing Around into his leadership practice.

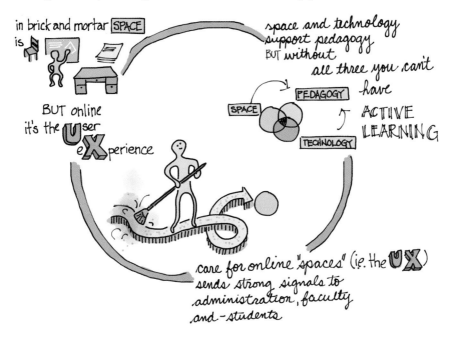

Good leaders visit the front lines; good blended leaders realize that the front lines are not always face to face.

WHERE THE FISH ARE

The frontlines are shifting dramatically right now. Walk into a true "Maker Space" and it's difficult to know where the instructor ends and the learner begins. Likewise, place-based education initiatives are shaking the very walls of the classroom.

Introducing a series of papers for Bank Street College of Education, guest editors Roberta Altman, Susan Stires, and Susan Weseen sound the alarm: "Across America, children are taught in classrooms that are judged increasingly by their adherence to common standards (in terms of appearance as well as content), by teachers who receive increasingly standardized training, and who are governed by imperatives that crowd out the possibility of paying attention to place. . . . This narrow, depleted classroom (a place in its own right) calls out for air—for opportunities" (Altman, Stires, & Weseen, 2015).

Outside of school, work is being transformed, as well. Walk into a thriving coworking space and you'll see dozens of motivated and engaged people sharing ideas, opening their networks to one another, swapping their phones for their iPads for their laptops for their notebooks, arriving at work when they choose to, leaving for the gym when they choose to, pursuing tasks with relentless focus one minute and laughing at an animated GIF the next. These spaces look more like bustling coffee shops than places where venture-backed and business-hardened startup CEOs mingle with fresh-out-of-college dreamers who might be holding the idea for the next big thing in their Moleskine notebooks. According to the research of Gretchen Spreitzer (University of Michigan's Ross School of Business), Lyndon Garrett (University of Michigan's Ross School of Business), and Peter Bacevice (senior design strategist with the New York office of HLW International), people thrive in coworking spaces because such spaces offer an ideal mix of autonomy—you can leave to exercise, you can stay to work—and for structure: "People need to be able to craft their work in ways that give them purpose and meaning. They should be given control and flexibility in their work environments" (Spreitzer et al., 2015, p. 30). It sounds like these places, properly equipped, would pass Greenleaf's test of servant leadership.

Outside of school, too, play is being transformed in ways that could, in turn, transform work. Have you ever watched young people "learn the ropes" in a complicated video game world? They don't need to be told what to do; they don't need to be "onboarded" or read an instruction manual; they process feedback rapidly and apply what they learn.

Is it any wonder, then, that spaces like Slack are being called the office of the future? As Scott Rosenberg points out in an article called "Shut Down Your Office. You Now Work in Slack," Slack, which has picked up millions of users (and millions of dollars in funding) in a rather short period of time, "almost demands a certain level of casual play" (Rosenberg, 2015). Slack's features (messaging, group conversations, attachments, API integrations) are not unique in the realm of productivity and communications platforms. What is unique is the way that Slack weaves these features together for seamless integration across multiple devices, providing app/dock notifications when there is something to which users need to pay attention. Slack works for people because it meets them where they work and it supports them in working the way they would like to work, tying them to digital spaces they can park in their pockets rather than physical spaces where they have to park themselves.

Leaders set the conditions for work, monitor them, adjust them as needed, and promote change in them when needed. Blended leaders, always on the lookout for the point of highest impact and greatest leverage, realize that you have to cast your line where the fish are. They don't stubbornly fish in the same nook because that's where they have always fished. And they don't try to force the fish to return to the old nook in order to be caught.

College admissions provides a good example. If you were charged with "selling" a college to a prospective student body, you would assume that your greatest asset would be the campus itself—the manicured lawns, the student spaces, the ancient trees, the immaculate buildings, the modernized dorms, flying Frisbees, the lake next door. . . . Yet Caylor Solutions recently released a summary of some key points from a student survey conducted with users of Chegg, an online textbook provider, and Uversity, a higher education data and communications platform. Here's what they found: 79 percent of students "reported that they would drop a school from consideration" if their experience of the school on the school's website did not meet their standards. And, 97 percent of the students surveyed reported that they consumed these websites via mobile devices (Caylor, 2014).

In principle, admissions directors have the same job they have always had—to attract and admit the right students—but their tactics must shift, much like the tactics of the US military, detailed in our introduction, had to shift when the state of modern warfare shifted. The same goes for school teachers and school leaders. Reshan stopped writing this book in order to care for the writing space of this book. He redefined his role for a few days to best serve the larger goal of the team. Sometimes you have to disrupt the default; sometimes you have to work in a different way; sometimes you have to add a different hat to an already crowded head.

Some of this thinking came from an analogous experience Steve had while working with a communication and marketing professional who helped him build a website for his school's May Term program (the same program that enabled Reshan to lead students in the entrepreneurial venture described at the start of this chapter). Steve felt that this program, which allows seniors to pursue independent projects, internships, or travel opportunities during the month of May, could benefit from having an online address to house resources, news, and media. He spent weeks building the website, writing the text, organizing photographs, and working closely with his school's director of technology. And then, when the site was launched, his school's director of communications called him and said, "Are you ready to get to work?"

Ready to get to work? Steve was ready to celebrate his work and move on to something else. But caring for a digital space like the May Term website (http://mayterm.mka.org) entails more than just dropping content into website templates; if you truly care about your content, you have to market it. You have to break off bits of it and send it to interested parties; you have to layer it across various social media platforms; you have to announce it both online and offline; you have to build your audience. And you have to keep adding content, linking to old content, connecting to other content.

It would have been easy for Steve to say, "That's not my job." But as a leader of a significant school program, one that will benefit offline from having robust support mechanisms online, Steve has to lead in thoroughly modern ways. He can delegate the work to others (say, an assistant in the communications office), but he has to truly understand what he is delegating so that he can envision what success will look like and adjust his practice if the website is not hitting its targets. The technology is important . . . but the person behind it is equally important. The leader must be enough of a technologist and enough of an editor-in-chief to help his followers thrive. As John Miller writes on http://www.scribewise.com, the editor in chief "for a content marketing effort must be committed to distribution. In this age of personalization, content creation must be done with an eye towards how the content will be consumed by the audience" (Miller, 2014).

All leaders know that marketing and resource gathering are important; blended leaders know exactly how technology can assist such efforts. They know their jobs are expanding, and they are willing to assume new roles if and when such roles help them to advance their projects and organizations.

BEYOND DESIGNING AND CARING FOR SPACES

Leaders who are technophobes and leaders who are technocrats will ultimately agree that designing for spaces and caring for spaces is important because caring for people is supremely important. Jonathan Ive, Apple's designer extraordinaire, considers "design thoughtfulness" a "sign of respect," and he speaks of his own encounters with well-designed space as "a feeling of gratitude that someone else actually thought this through in a way that makes your life easier" (Parker, 2015).

So if you follow the beliefs in this chapter and find yourself frustratingly tangled up in digital space, return to the noble purpose of such work: ensuring your followers have what they need to do their jobs well, ensuring your followers are "freer, more autonomous." Organizing digital spaces can be mucky work. Slogging through the unedited thinking of others requires concentration and stamina. But someone has to do it, bring shape to it, follow up with it. Someone has to lead in this area.

There's a tension in the app developer community that provides a useful analogy. You have noticed that apps always ask to be updated. This happens whether you ask for the update or not.

If you were caring for those spaces (caring for those apps), you would have to decide if you wanted them to be "reverse compatible" or if you wanted to press your users to change their behaviors. Making an app reverse compatible involves catering to the lowest common denominator environment (that is, the slowest processor speeds, the lowest memory capacity, and the worst graphics). The upside is that reverse compatible apps will work on old devices and that old behaviors do not need to change. On the other hand, the developer who pushes his or her app forward, making it accessible only on the latest, greatest machines and software, generates the best possible user experience. However, what worked fine yesterday will no longer work today.

The moral of the story? Sometimes, you can only make your app, or your online/offline space, do amazing things if you are willing to push people to upgrade their software/apps/habits. The developer has a responsibility to guide the user to the update, acknowledging a behavior shift. But those who make such a change without warning or steps for mediation are not leading well. They are caring for spaces without caring for users.

So as you approach your work in online spaces, decide if you are going to use a space in a way that will work for everyone or if you need your teams to upgrade their own engagement, their own interaction. Fortunately, there are some simple operating procedures to ensure that spaces are forward updated and users are cared for.

1. When change is coming, announce it in advance—give people lead time to know about it (for example, "We'll be updating our interface, and here is a preview").
2. Once the update has happened, provide steps toward becoming updated (Please update your [browser, OS, and so on]).
3. Make the update worth it. If you want users to trust you even when an unexpected (though advertised) roadblock emerges, you have a responsibility for the update to be better than what you had before.

We have come a long way from IKEA boxes and garbage cans in class-rooms, and at the same time, we have not moved past the simple lessons of those stories. Blended leaders design and care for spaces. This work is not always glamorous or obvious—it is foundational. In a technology-drenched world, you have to lead online well to lead offline well. You have to update resources when need be and help people continue to engage with, and uncover, the value of technological spaces. You have to give people what they need to do amazing work.

BELIEFS IN PRACTICE: THINGS TO TRY #2

An Offline Thing

Visit a retail store in a nearby town or neighborhood. Before you go in, think about something you are pretty sure that store would sell but that you don't know where it would be located or how it is priced. Then go into the store and find the item. How long did it take you to locate the item? Did anyone help you find it? Did you stop to look at other things while looking for the first thing? What could be changed in the store to improve your experience? Is it something related to the physical layout of the space? Could interactions with the staff have made a difference?

An Online Thing

Use either the same item from the previous task (but not necessarily the same retail store) or a new item for this task. Go online and locate it. How many keystrokes, clicks, and/or taps did it take you to get to the item? Did you use a generic search engine or a search bar on a store website? Did you learn about any other products while locating yours? How many additional keystrokes, clicks, and/or taps would be needed to get that item delivered to your doorstep? Did auto-fill play a role at any point? Did using a phone instead of a laptop or tablet make a difference?

A Blended Thing

At your next meeting or any other event where you and others will be listening to or engaging in discussions for more than 30 minutes in the same room, invite two other colleagues who are present to take group notes together in a shared Google Document. After the meeting has concluded, within one week, go back and organize the collective notes using headers, topics and subtopics, consistent style formatting, and coherent sentence or note structure. Share this curated document (in Comments Only mode) with all other attendees of the meeting or event, including the speaker, inviting them to leave comments either in response to, or in order to improve, the shared notes.

Photo by Modestas Urbonas

BELIEF #3

BLENDED LEADERS REJECT INSULARITY AND EMBRACE SHARING

RIDING WITH TOM NAMMACK

Within Steve's first month as a new (very green) school administrator, he attended a conference with several other (much more seasoned) administrators from his school. The team was trying to gather information about a potential new program, and we had found a well-regarded annual conference that specialized in the topic.

Thrown in without a net and without much context, Steve tried to find ways to contribute once his team hit the ground. Wandering from session to session, though, he did not find much. He picked speakers the way he might have picked horses at a racetrack—by studying the program and observing the speakers as they warmed up before their sessions. By the end of the conference, Steve's method left him with a handful of bum tickets and no payoff. He had only a vague sense of what he would share when the admin team regrouped at school the following week. He figured he would say something about how the conference was unsatisfying or how the speakers were unprepared or uninspiring. He would talk, in other words, about how and why the conference didn't fully meet his needs.

For the ride home, he jumped in with his school's headmaster, Tom Nammack. As Tom turned the car onto the highway, and what became known in Steve's mind as the "journey of a thousand questions" began, Steve had a vague sense as to why the other administrators had opted for the train. Tom asked Steve a question about the conference, Steve responded, and for much of the car ride that followed, this pattern repeated. Tom asked; Steve answered. Tom wanted to know about Steve's experiences in the classroom teaching English, about his experiences as an advisor, about his opinion on certain school policies, about his family and interests and goals.

When Tom stopped to fill up for gas, Steve bought the biggest coffee he could find. Back in the car, the first hit of caffeine fortified him; the second made him realize that something wonderfully counterintuitive was happening. Though Tom was not answering any of the questions, Steve was getting to know him by listening to the kinds—and volume—of questions he asked.

The questions revealed Tom's curiosity; also, though, they revealed his passion for uncovering what he does not know and cannot see. They revealed a restless mind fond of testing reality, triangulating data, measuring gaps between mission and practice, adding—always adding—new dashes of color, new flashes of detail, to his internal map of the school for which he is ultimately responsible.

The questions also revealed Tom's humility. To close the gaps in your understanding the way Tom was willing to, one has to first admit that such gaps exist. One has to first admit that he does not, in fact, have all the territories mapped.

Curiosity, passion for inquiry, and humility: these qualities would have served Steve well at his first conference as an administrator. Though his career was several decades younger than Tom Nammack's, Steve was operating like someone who thought he was supposed to know everything—and therefore, someone unwilling to ask the right questions at the right times, unwilling to pull aside conference speakers, unwilling to let down his guard or to prepare properly by examining the gaps in his knowledge.

Nearly a decade after his car ride with Tom, Steve noticed that Tom still wields the artful, well-timed question as one of his primary learning and leading tools, reinventing it as opportunities arise. His method has allowed him to manage and lead a deeply complex institution through endlessly choppy waters: the subprime mortgage crisis that made plenty of people wonder if they could afford private school; the moment when laptops and other devices become de facto parts of day-to-day school life; the transition of marketing from art to science; the influence of Facebook, Twitter, and Snapchat on communication; the call for global educational opportunities to be folded into one's local educational opportunities; the moment when diversity and inclusion initiatives became central to the work we do in schools. Tom has served his school well by being clear that he could not possibly know all the answers to all the questions school would ask and by opening his school—continually—to the world of ideas beyond his school. In refusing the insularity of "old school" private schools, Tom Nammack serves as an example of the post–"lone warrior," post–John Wayne-style school leader described by Pearl Rock Kane in her now-classic article referenced in our introduction (Kane, 1998).

And, what's more, he doesn't seem likely to change. Recently, he started a tradition of meeting privately with every outgoing senior advisor group. When Steve asked him what he did during those meetings, he said, "Mostly I just ask questions."

"Like?" Steve asked. (He, too, had learned something.)

"What escapes our notice?" Tom asked. "What do we need to know that we aren't currently seeing?"

THE BUSINESS CASE FOR HUMILITY
OR $Q + BA = (I)^2$

Tom Nammack is humble by nature, and this humility has allowed him to thrive in a leadership context wherein humility is not just a nice-to-have but also a bona fide need-to-have. Creativity expert Warren Berger, who wrote a definitive book on the way questions spark innovation, writes, "Whereas in the past one needed to appear to have 'all the answers' in order to rise in companies, today, at least in some enlightened segments of the business world, the corner office is for the askers" (Berger, 2014, p. 5).

His book, *A More Beautiful Question: The Power of Inquiry to Spark Breakthrough Ideas,* as well as several other recent books including *Little Bets*, mentions how great questioners lead some of the most admired companies of the twenty-first century, such as Amazon, Google, and Apple. And, as Clayton Christensen (2014) writes in the foreword to *Blended*,

BE HUMBLE

YOU WILL NEED THE
GRACE OF OTHERS
BECAUSE YOU ARE GOING TO DISRUPT
THEIR LIVES.

AND EVEN IF THAT'S A GOOD THING
THAT'S A REALLY BIG ASK.

channeling Thomas Kuhn, the humble approach can actually topple traditions and paradigms—can actually lead to serious, world-bending innovation:

> *Often, only a theory that is used in another branch of science in which the original and deepest believers of the paradigm have little background can help reveal . . . pattern across [its] anomalies. Because of this, the devout defend the validity of the original paradigm, often to their graves. Indeed, their instinctive toolkit that they used for learning in their branch of science renders many of them unable to see the anomalies that put the paradigm into question. For this reason, Kuhn observed that new researchers, whose training and disciplines are different, typically initiate the toppling of a paradigm and the development of the new knowledge that takes its place. (Christensen, 2014, p. xvi)*

In some sense, new researchers create disruptive innovation because they are naïve enough to ask questions that expert researchers would never, ever ask—indeed, questions that might cause fellow experts to laugh them out of the room. What we are really getting at here, then, is the power of the growth mindset as applied to leadership. Leaders with fixed mindsets hide behind incomplete knowledge or hold up a veneer of truth. Leaders with growth mindsets know that they couldn't possibly lead effectively, especially for long periods of time, without asking for help.

To put an even finer point on it, leaders have no excuse to misjudge their own capacities. Sure, we've known since Oedipus that we can miss our blind spots, even when they become very obvious. But that's just a story, right? The pioneering work of Daniel Kahneman, who won a Nobel Prize in Economics, proves the story true. His colleague Steven Pinker writes of Kahneman: "[Kahneman's] central message could not be more important, namely, that human reason left to its own devices is apt to engage in a number of fallacies and systematic errors, so if we want to make better decisions in our personal lives and as a society, we ought to be aware of these biases and seek workarounds" (Pinker, 2014). Effective leaders today know that asking questions, or seeking feedback, helps us to see our blind spots. Hubris (the opposite of humility) powers us toward possible ruin; humility (the opposite of hubris) guides us back, keeping us focused and flexible and open to workarounds, such as the artful, humble question.

If you examine, again, the blended leader, the one who capitalizes on affordances made by control of "time, path, place, and/or pace," you will see a leader perfectly situated to thrive in a world where the spoils go to the questioners. Blended leaders are the opposite of the leaders who, in having only a hammer, treat every problem like a nail (surely, we have all been on the receiving end of such leaders' problem-solving approach). Blended leaders, on the contrary, keep lots of tools—whether online or offline—in their toolkits because they are never quite sure which one they will need. What is more, they leave room in their toolkits in case they have to learn how to use a brand-new tool when faced with a problem they have not seen—or solved well—before.

Blended leaders' collaborative patterns parallel their use of a wide variety of tools. Rather than going directly to the default—that is, the hammer—they seek proper tools only after understanding problems properly and thoroughly. Likewise, they are willing to bypass the "right" collaborators in favor of finding the best collaborators. There is quite a difference. The *right* collaborators have the right titles, fit in the right place in the hierarchy, have the right degrees from the right colleges, and usually have the right to speak first, foremost, and with unquestioned authority. The *best* collaborators might happen to be those people, but they can also be anyone who can offer honest insight, creative perspective, a willingness to embrace failure, and an insistence on play and iteration in search of viable solutions. They can be old or young, new or experienced, in or out of network, in or out of the discipline within which the problem is framed.

Blended leaders can bypass familiar knowledge channels because they know they can go anywhere—quickly, and at any time—to find help. They know that, as Einstein reputedly said, you should not expect to solve problems with the same mind that created them. If your go-to team's standard operating procedure made a mess, perhaps the procedure itself was to blame and perhaps they aren't the best team to understand what caused the mess.

Blended leaders also favor opening their iterative process, their inquiry, to others. They know they don't profit by keeping trade secrets; they profit, instead, by feeding into, and off of, learning channels. Admittedly, their approach is inflected with a software maker's ethos. As Paul Ford wrote in "What Is Code?" his epic, 38,000 word *Bloomberg Business* essay, "Software is everywhere. It's gone from a craft of fragile, built-from-scratch custom projects to an industry of standardized parts, where coders absorb and improve upon the labors of their forebears (even if those forebears are one cubicle over)" (Ford, 2015).

Scott Berkun expands on this notion of "absorbing and improving" in *The Year without Pants*, the story of WordPress. Berkun shows how Matt Mullenweg, early in the development of the company that would become WordPress, turned a dead lead into a solution that changed the Internet (and therefore the world). Barely a high school graduate, Mullenweg was trying to solve a problem related to photography, but the program he was using—Cafelog—had stopped serving his needs. The person driving it had literally disappeared. Most of us in this situation would settle for one of two choices: continuing to use the program in a suboptimal way, or finding another program. Mullenweg chose a third way, in this case the way of the programmer. Berkun explains:

> *While most software is copyrighted and closed, Cafelog had different rules. It did not have a copyright. Instead it had something called an open source license, or a copyleft. This meant anyone could copy the source code for Cafelog and do what they wanted with it, including making a competitor to Cafelog (that copy is known as a fork, as in a fork in the road). The wrinkle was that anyone who did this would have to use the same license in whatever they made—a little rule that had a grand implication: it ensured that ideas inside software could live on and be useful in ways the original creator never imagined. (Berkun, 2013, p. 30)*

Mullenweg was the beneficiary of Cafelog's passion for ideas and openness. In turn, he had to abide by those same principles. Blended leaders watch, and learn from, these benevolent cycles. As they develop solutions or processes, they want to share them with others—they want to practice a kind of open source leadership, saying, essentially, "My victory is your new platform." Ultimately, the sense that others in their school—or in the educational field—might be able to use their breadcrumb trail to find their own way is a good thing, because new journeys clear new pathways for teachers to teach (and learn) and students to learn (and grow).

The question is not why anyone would want to lead in a blended way, it is why would anyone not want to lead in a blended way? Technology, even very simple technology, offers options to extend good instincts and scale good intentions. Let us return to Tom Nammack for a moment. Tom Nammack is a headmaster. There is one of him at each private school (and sometimes he is a she). His job gives him the opportunity, the gift, to lead in the way he sees fit. And others, like Steve and Reshan, have a chance to learn from him. But others, like Steve and Reshan, do not need to wait to assume Tom Nammack's mantle to begin to apply what they learn from him, especially in a world that offers so many tools to carry out his particular leadership legacy. Blended leadership enables us to practice and model the kinds of humility, the kinds of questioning, that reduce our reliance on our own egos, our own cognitive biases, our traditional ways of doing things, our unquestioned default settings, a closed approach.

In *A More Beautiful Question*, Berger presents a formula: "Q (questioning) + A (action) = I (innovation)" (Berger, 2014). We would add that, in schools, you can also multiply A by B (blended leadership) to increase innovative outcomes exponentially: $Q + BA = (I)^2$. To see some examples of the formula in action, we need to jump from the theoretical perch we've been balancing on to an anthropological perch: real teachers in, and out of, real schools.

ASKING OLD QUESTIONS TO NEW PEOPLE

Successful blended leaders accept the fact that they don't know everything, and often, they are willing to broadcast that fact in an effort to get the answers they need. At the same time, they take seriously the ways in which technology can connect them to outside problem solvers or, in Christensen's words, new researchers.

This way of working and leading contrasts sharply with the traditional mode of leadership, wherein the leader is seen as the unified and authoritative voice, the one who has the answers, the one who is unshakeable in the face of a crisis and expresses doubts only privately and with a limited number of people.

Blended leaders may very well be unshakeable, but they work—by choice—in a tangle of voices and ideas, mediated by their primary workstation (that is, their computing device). Tweets, texts, emails, and instant messages roll in continuously, informing the blended leader's thoughts and actions. What looks like a distracted and fragmented world of work gains clarity when you understand the simple credo that drives it: Blended leaders believe that connected brains are more powerful than unconnected brains, that more brains are better than fewer when solving complex problems or dealing with a world, technological or otherwise, that changes continually.

The book in front of you, from its earliest stages, was meant to exemplify this credo and show an example of its possible outputs. It was drafted and designed by two individuals using one of Google's cloud services. We knew that we would both bring different skills and ideas to the project, and that together we would be much more prone to say something of value than we would on our own. The book unfolded as a continual back-and-forth process, with each author regularly asking the other for help.

Writing collaboratively in a document nested in the cloud, and with an openness to the voices just clicks away from that document, moves one past the notion of the solitary author or solitary thinker. You start a sentence that your collaborator might complete, altering your original intention in unexpected ways. As you are writing, your collaborator might drop a comment alongside your paragraph, redirecting your thoughts, asking for clarification, or adding a new fact. As you are writing, you might leave a thought unfinished and insert a question as a comment that will then show up as an alert on your collaborator's phone. Meanwhile, if you leave your tabs open, you can shift rapidly between a host of tools that can help you to shape and advance your ideas: Gmail for longer-term questions, Twitter for immediate feedback, an online dictionary for nuance, online research for depth or support.

Sure, it is possible to call this writing experience "distracted," but we prefer to call it "network informed." Solitary writing and thinking has its place, but the solitary writer and thinker has more options than ever before, built right into his or her computing device, to ask for help, to seek wider contexts for his or her thoughts. So that's one reason we partnered. The book itself is an artifact reflecting how one might learn, think, and lead as a result of the interconnectedness of computing devices.

BUILDING SMALL PUBLIC WORK GROUPS

At one point, early on, we decided to push the "asking for help" principle by starting a Twitter chat to see how other online leaders felt about the work they were doing. We chose Twitter as a medium because we knew it would attract leaders who were already comfortable operating in online environments. And we didn't once mention the conversation outside an online environment.

We simply publicized it (quickly and painlessly, we might add) via Twitter and our respective blogs. A few people helped in the publicity by retweeting our message to their own followers. Then we "showed up" at the stated time and started with a question: "How do leaders ask for help in an online world?"

For the next hour, a half-dozen contributors—from North Carolina, Illinois, New Jersey, and New York City—talked about how, when, and why they ask for help. A few of us had met before, but some of us were talking for the first time. What follows is a close reading of parts of the conversation, performed to extract its value.

At one point, the conversation turned to different levels of faculty engagement with online resources: as more faculty members at our schools engage in continuous conversations outside their schools, conversations that are happening online, the nature of the dialogue within our schools will necessarily change. To punctuate this conversation, Bill Stites, director of technology at Montclair Kimberley Academy, shared a resource from Scott Rocco, a superintendent from New Jersey. Rocco's post, for edSocialMedia, depicted the ways in which faculty members can move from watching social media conversations to shaping and extending those dialogues.

You might be thinking, "A guy shared a link. That's no big deal." That's a fair point, but let's dig into the gesture a little bit. It was not just a guy sharing a link. It was a guy sharing the right link at the right time in the right place.

Unpacked: the importance of Stites's share grows if you look at it from the perspective of leading and learning. Because Bill shared a post in the context of a particular conversation, with the conversant individuals seeking particular information and insight, and because Bill shared a resource at the precise moment that the participants could best learn from it, he added value to a link that, until then, was idly posted on a website like millions of other links.

So the forum itself, the Twitter chat, set up quickly and executed effortlessly, intensified the value of the common share as well as the link being shared. It also led to a consideration of Google Plus, a social network. Is it ready for primetime at our schools? Is it ready to be used as a collaborative tool to help school faculties learn from each other and "ask for help"?

Reshan and Jason Ramsden, chief technology officer at Ravenscroft School, answered the questions in the same way: "Not yet." Jason shared his investigations into using private communities in Google Plus for internal conversations. Reshan share that the Web interface had gotten too busy for him, but that the iPad version and the Hangouts video conferencing feature of G+ were both positive elements.

Here we have two technology leaders who not only have influence over the professional development agendas of their schools, but also have influence over others at other schools. Put more simply, if Reshan or Jason thinks something is a good idea, other tech leaders are going to take note. And if Reshan and Jason think something is not quite ripe, then others are going to slow down in their own investment in the product or service. Plus, these two leaders have reaffirmed each other's thinking.

So in the end, the group who assembled for our first Twitter chat shared some resources, talked about their use of an emerging tool (Google Plus), coached each other a bit, challenged each other's thinking, and then went back to their lives. What's more, some old friends reconnected, some weak ties became stronger, and some new relationships were born—all in a quick hour's work from the comfort of our own homes.

The conversation itself was saved on Storify, an approachable tool for archiving Twitter conversations. Though not every (and probably not most) Twitter chats deserve such revered status, some conversations, like the one that was just described, become learning discourses. Any participant can access the conversation to remind him or herself (What was that article that Bill Stites recommended?) or to reflect (as we did earlier) or to lean on the perspective of an expert (What was Jason Ramsden saying about Google Plus? Maybe I should reach out to him as my school seeks to explore this new medium?).

We hope the lengthy detour into a meta-analysis of our own writing and collaborative process now seems justified in the context of our larger points. By setting up the chat, we (Reshan and Steve) attempted to lead the learning of others. By opening ourselves to the conversation and its potential value, we learned as a result of leading. Any school leader with a connection to the Internet could use this same method to solve a knotty problem—building a small public work group to surface fresh solutions, to gather perspectives from people who weren't involved with the creation of the problem or who, more important, haven't internalized the perceived limitations of the organization. (We have a simple rule that we call "the rule of 12": If everyone in the faculty room is telling you that something can't be done, ask a dozen strangers before you give up on the idea.)

BUILDING, AND CONTRIBUTING TO, LARGE PUBLIC WORK GROUPS

Because of our iterative approach, Steve and Reshan were lucky enough to take the ideas in this book on the road often. From the earliest inception of our ideas—notes on the back of hotel notepads—to the book you are holding, we spoke in more than a dozen venues to many different kinds of audiences. Our goals when speaking at conferences were always the same—not only to inform and entertain our audiences, but also to learn from them.

The setup of conferences makes the latter part of this task difficult, even when you set up collaborative note-taking spaces to try to join people together and solicit their opinions. After a session, too, most people are usually moving on to something else, and the people who stick around are generally positive rather than constructively critical.

The best workout our ideas ever had happened when we were at our respective homes, sipping our respective Saturday morning coffee, wearing our respective pajamas. Scott Rocco had invited us to host something called #satchat. It's a pretty simple concept; educators from around the world tweet about certain topics using the hashtag #satchat to connect the tweets. When you're only keeping half an eye on the space, it's pleasant; when you're trying to moderate it, it's like a hyped-up version of Space Invaders where what flies at you—and often past you—are comments, links, jokes, and questions about pedagogy, educational practice, books, articles, apps, programs, and so on.

After an hour of asking people to respond to our beliefs, many of which are discussed in this book, we had heard from 394 active participants who shared 441 links, 2,324 unique tweets, and 694 retweets. In the moment, all of this was a little overwhelming. Combing back through the conversation, though, there's a lot there—a lot of leads to pursue, a lot of actionable ideas, a lot of new thinkers to follow.

What follows is just a small sample of what we took from our #satchat experience and how it flexed our ideas.

We launched our first question: Effective leaders today not only lead the learning of others, but lead by learning. In what ways do you lead *by* learning?

One of the first replies came from @hayhurst, a teacher who described how she videotaped her own coaching sessions to better understand her practice. She publicly conceded her discomfort with the taping aspect, but she qualified her reaction by pointing out that such a practice is part of her learning and growth. @ScottRRocco, a #satchat cofounder, described a monthly staff newsletter he produced and shared a link to an example.

We posed our second question: We believe effective leaders ask for help but, more important, accept help. How have you accepted help recently?

@bradmcurrie, another #satchat cofounder, shared how a specific tool, Voxer, helped with a problem that was not unique to his school. He stated that educators in his state were struggling with implementing certain standardized tests. They used the tool to share tips and tricks.

Our third question followed: How have you used, or seen others use, online tools to extend or articulate the missions of organizations?

@MathDenisNJ referenced another educator (@NMHS_lms) while also invoking an additional hashtag (#makerspace) where he was seeing mission articulation happening. @cybraryman1 suggested posting the mission on the school website, blog, and regular communications and then shared a link to his own curated resources around this topic. @jvincentsen shared her school's evidence of mission articulation while remarking that the branding of it was a work in progress. Interesting to us (in a good way) is how something publicly available and important as a mission can have the words "work in progress" associated with one form of its articulation. These were just a small fraction of the responses to only a few of the questions we posed that morning.

So how does this happen? It helps that the #satchat audience is boldly participatory. They share without shyness and ask for help when they need it. They are comfortable sharing successes, setbacks, and works in progress. And the whole event moves so quickly that most participants—the ones who are adding to the conversation rather than passively watching it— throw out their gut reactions, their intuitive responses, to whatever they happen to see. Such candor is often lost in face-to-face meetings where— especially in schools—people tend to avoid conflict or awkwardness.

But the whole endeavor is also set up very deliberately and thoughtfully. If you moderate a discussion, the organizers—Billy, Brad, and Scott—ask you to submit questions weeks in advance, making sure you have constructed questions that will work for the group. Going back to Berger, there should be no surprise that such innovative sharing practices—and the flood of innovative ideas that follow—would be spurred by such a carefully calibrated questioning process.

If there were a Hall of Fame for blended leaders, the leaders behind #satchat would be in it. They promote shared humility in the face of problems that are too complex for any one leader or one school to solve. And they scale such work by tying teachers together with computers, networks, and hashtags. Their project is simple, elegant, useful, and constrained (in the best sense of the word), and it all happens outside the school building and the school week.

MORE ABOUT #SATCHAT

We interviewed the founders of #satchat in June 2015.

RESHAN RICHARDS: Can you give us a history of #satchat? Why did you start it? What was the goal or hunch?

SATCHAT FOUNDERS (Scott Rocco, Brad Currie, Billy Krakower): In 2012 Brad and [Scott] connected on Twitter and began to discuss the idea of creating an educational chat. Both of us were looking to create something that was positive and progressive and available for future and current administrators. This concept of positive and progressive and available was missing from traditional education conversations at the time. So we debated the idea of having a Saturday morning discussion group through Twitter called #Satchat. We also agreed to have it at 7:30 a.m. but felt the number of educators interested in joining might be limited by the fact that it was a Saturday and so early in the morning. There were twenty-five educators on the first #satchat and over the past few years it has grown to hundreds. The chat has also transitioned from only current and future administrators to all kinds of current and future educators.

RR: Can you talk about the current format of #satchat (for example, the way in which you drive the conversation by planting questions in the Twitter stream)? How and why did you settle on this format?

SF: The format has not changed much since the first discussion. We start with a welcome and then ask participants to introduce themselves, where they are from, and what their position is as an educator. It is interesting to see where people are joining. We have had people from all over the world. We then ask six questions during the remaining time. The format seems to work well for the conversation and flow of ideas.

RR: We feel that the people behind #satchat are representative of a new kind of leader—a leader who is willing to promote shared vulnerability and humility in the face of problems that are too complex for any one leader or one school to solve. Do you agree with this contextualization of #satchat? Is there anything you would add to it?

SF: It has created an environment where your thoughts (tweets) are professional but have a very personal attachment. In addition to tweeting, your actions need to support what you put out there because people are now following you. I think it is creating leaders who are willing to support change in education, those who might not normally have a voice, and provide opportunities for people to collaborate who would never have the opportunity without technology.

PUBLIC TROUBLESHOOTING: USER BASE AND BRAND

Our experiences setting up our own Twitter chats and participating in #satchat have shown us that leaders can and should use the technological forums available to them to ask others for help, to listen to many voices rather than simply a chosen few, and to lead with "multiple tabs open." All these moves help them avoid insularity at a time when being open, available, and accepting is less a choice than an imperative.

All these moves also help them to build a new kind of relationship with their users (that is, their constituents). We can turn again to Twitter (and the startup world) to see how pointed, real-time feedback can project and protect a brand's identity while fortifying the user's experience with that brand.

At Explain Everything, Reshan's company that provides the interactive whiteboard and screencasting application of the same name, if someone posts a question on Twitter that the company knows is very specific to the user's situation, requires additional personal information from the user, or is too complex to summarize in a few tweets, Reshan will often just reply with, "Can you please email support@explaineverything.com? We can help you better there!" Most people do follow up this way.

However, many times when users post questions or comments on Twitter, Reshan and his company feel that they have a unique opportunity. Responding to the queries in a timely manner gives users the "just-in-time" support they want, which is not always possible with email, and shows them that the company is actively listening.

Also, responding to users on Twitter makes the question and its answer visible to all the users' followers (and followers of any chat hashtags they may include). If someone from the Explain Everything team is not in a position to write back right away, perhaps someone outside the company may know the answer. The entire user base (like the entire #satchat audience) becomes a potent ally, and if they love the company, they are happy to help.

A company willing to truly meet individual users where they are, and empower members of its user base to help one another, builds a unique relationship with its customers. Individuals know they can interact with the entire brand—not only an individual or small team within the brand. The ability to engage in this kind of exchange elevates the brand beyond its component parts while also elevating the importance of the user and that user's experience. The company is saying, in a way, "Your work, and the problems it surfaces, is our work. Our future, as a company, will be tied to your work, as an individual."

USER SUPPORT: A NETWORKED VERSION

Here's an example of a typical Twitter exchange between an Explain Everything user, someone following her on Twitter, and Explain Everything:

Sylvia Duckworth, a wonderful world language teacher from Canada, makes her learning and leading visible by sharing her work and activities on Twitter. She recently reached out to Explain Everything because she was having trouble with a "grouping" feature. In her initial message, she also cc'd her friend and fellow Google Certified Teacher Jennie Magiera.

Reshan happened to be online at the time and responded to the tweet right away by first attempting to clarify the exact steps Sylvia was taking. After her next reply, Reshan asked additional questions about her hardware and systems and suggested an alternative that Sylvia could use while they figured out why the other method was seemingly not working for her.

In the meantime, Amy Brewis, another Explain Everything user, chimed in to say that she didn't know about the feature which Sylvia was asking about and then tried it out. When the new—to her—method worked, she declared that she'd bring it back to her students. Amy might be a follower of Sylvia, or of Explain Everything, or of both, but the public interaction between Sylvia and Explain Everything led to the "discovery" of something new for her. Sylvia closed the loop with Amy by acknowledging her comment and also suggesting possible reasons for the problem with which she had been grappling. Through the online discourse with Amy and Reshan, Sylvia discovered that she was doing the steps incorrectly.

Within a matter of minutes, Sylvia's problem was solved, another educator was able to learn something new, and a company was able to publicly demonstrate how it troubleshoots problems and does its best to help all users. It is entirely likely that, seeing this exchange, other people might be encouraged to reach out to the company this way or to even download the app. The entire conversation is archived on Twitter and searchable, so that if another user has the same problem, Reshan or someone from Explain Everything can share the dialogue (as he has here) or quickly replicate the solution.

Imagine if your school could engage its constituents in the same fashion, breaking down traditional communication channels, solidifying the school's position on certain things, helping people in real time. Many schools have Twitter handles that represent their brands (or help them tell the story of student learning in their schools), but these handles still sit at some distance from the real action. They deliver official pronouncements and steady streams of approved media, much like old-school press agents. Such use is fine, it's a step, but it represents only a small slice of what is possible in terms of communication, community building, and brand amplification made possible by organizations willing to expose and troubleshoot their flaws in public.

TROUBLEFINDING AND TROUBLESHOOTING: BEYOND TWITTER

Another way to access a wide range of voices and perspectives, one that works for a leader-learner who wants something slower and more methodical, is the listserv.

When Reshan is presented with a question or challenge, he sometimes wants to access the perspectives of people from outside his institution before constructing or delivering his own response. He generally starts by sending a query to the NYCIST ListServ.

Reshan's first job at a school was being a fifth-grade math teacher and an assistant in the technology department at a small independent school in New York City. His boss and mentor informed him about a group of people in the area who had formed an email distribution list (listserv) on which they shared information and asked questions. During his first three years, Reshan used to go back and forth between subscribing and unsubscribing to this group, mostly because he was a passive participant and many of the conversations seemed like noise to him.

A few years later, this group's size and activity grew at the same rate that educational technology was increasingly present on people's radars, and Reshan found that the collective and contextual knowledge of the group could often be more reliable than any Google search or external consultant for that matter.

So when he has a question, he posts it to this group. Usually within the day he has anywhere from five to ten solid responses or follow-up questions. Not everyone replies to every email, but he is certain that a majority of this group reads the messages (or at least the subject lines) before deleting.

What is more, every question posted on a discussion forum becomes permanent evidence of both gaps in knowledge and an ability to seek ways to fill those gaps. With a quick search of a Google Group he belongs to, Reshan can find more than five years worth of documented knowledge gaps in the form of requests for help to do the job he was technically being paid to do. Participating in such a forum may seem like a risk, because he was simultaneously exposing these gaps and requests for help to people who may be future bosses or who may someday be competing for the same job as he is.

In the past, fear of this risk may have been appropriate. However, this breadcrumb trail does not lead to a represented lack of knowledge but rather reveals one's grasp of how to solve problems by relying on a network of people who have similar contexts and experiences. It reveals a self-starting, growth-oriented mindset. Certainly you learn a lot by doing—by trying to solve problems without any additional help. But, when others (or an entire institution) are relying on you to find the solution to a problem, such fumbling around in the dark may be a luxury.

Another advantage of such a public display of gaps in knowledge is that it makes available other people's public questioning practices. Of course many online discussion participants are hidden behind identity-fogging avatars and usernames, but when Googling a solution, the best answer often comes not from officials from a product or service but rather from engaged users on message boards—from "new researchers," passionate amateurs, and the newly converted.

BUG BOUNTY

Some companies are willing to pay to find flaws (especially security flaws) in their software. They are willing to pay, in other words, to develop a habit in their user base—"Find a flaw and tell us about it and we'll give you something in return." "Bug bounty" programs, as they are known, reframe subversive behavior (hacking into systems to see where they are broken) in order to help companies fulfill their missions, embrace the knowledge, experience, and skillset of curious users and hackers, and make the ongoing development of their product a participatory process.

An ethos of continuous learning emerges; companies that promote bug bounties announce that their work is forever unfinished. And they announce that they care about their wider community of users. Bug bounties enable people who can break the system and disrupt the lives of users to support the system, and in turn, the lives of users. Buying into such a program, from a company standpoint, requires a swapping out of ego for a commitment to learning and service.

We recently asked a few tech companies to share their thinking behind their bug bounty programs. A representative from Avast! Antivirus software and the community manager for Prezi both shared some interesting insights, reflecting the kind of growth mindset that we often talk about in schools.

BUG BOUNTY INTERVIEWS

Why did you launch a Bug Bounty program?

UNNAMED EMPLOYEE, AVAST! ANTIVIRUS SOFTWARE: As a security company, we want our product to be as secure as possible. We also understand that any software may contain bugs—the fact that the software or the company deals with security doesn't make it an exception. So we wanted to draw attention of other security experts to our products and motivate them to search for vulnerabilities—so that we can fix them.

CSABA FAIX, COMMUNICATIONS MANAGER AT PREZI: We, at Prezi, made a strategic decision in 2013 to shut down our QA department. We decided to change the workflow within Prezi and the QA became part of every team's job. Our philosophy was that the engineers should not only code but test the product as well. To allow users to test our services is common in the industry and we did not have a QA team anymore, and although our security team continuously keeps an eye on our product we decided to launch a Bug Bounty program as an extra safety net. The program allows [our security team] to receive a lot of feedback from ethical hackers so we can pay attention to the strength and weaknesses of our system. It helps us to be aware of potential weakness and be ready to answer them 24/7 with state of the art knowledge. Our security team in the meantime shares this knowledge in-house, making it available for every Prezi engineer.

What do you think this program says about your company culture?

UE: First, we are confident about the quality of our products, so we are not afraid to offer rewards for bugs discovered. Second, we are happy to work with the community (be it the community of security researchers in this case, or the community of our users in other cases).

CF: It tells a lot about how open and transparent we are. Having a public program which calls others to test our product for vulnerabilities also [articulates] our approach [to] failing. We acknowledge if something is not right instead of hiding it. This program [provides] evidence of this value.

Is the program working?

UE: Yes, it is working. Over the past two years, we have fixed about fifty reported security issues. Of course, some of the bugs could have been discovered internally or fixed as side effects of other improvements during the time, but the Bug Bounty program made it possible to fix them faster, and cover a wider area of possible problems.

CF: Yes. We truly believe that to find the best way you need to fail and learn from it.

Finally, is there an example of a bug that was reported and had a big impact on strategy or company direction?

UE: No, not really. The reported bugs were mostly technical issues— missing checks or validations, bypassing the protection using a path we didn't think of, options that were available for everybody even though they should have been accessible to administrators only. No reported bug required significant changes in the product design or changes in the overall strategy.

CF: [Recently] a security vulnerability was found by a bug hunter, and although we fixed it, he came back a few days later [saying] that he still would be able to exploit the issue. We fixed [it] once again and published a blog post [explaining the situation]. A few hours later some of those who read the blog post realized that, based on the code snippets we shared, our fix could still be bypassed with some more advanced tricks. This story has two learnings. First, that you always learn. And second is that we have to learn not only how to fix issues, but also to think like hackers—to use a completely different mindset while we are developing our product.

Details of the story of the bug hunter can be found at https://medium.com/prezi-engineering/prezi-got-pwned-a-tale-of-responsible-disclosure-ccdc71bb6dd1.

Here's an irony to consider: Schools are engines designed to promote learning and growth. And yet, we sometimes have a hard time selling ourselves as organizations that are in a state of continual growth. Parents often love new programs or curriculum, but they would prefer that the associated growing pains, the inevitable stumbles, happen off set, away from the children. "Grow all you want—and yes please grow a lot," they seem to suggest, "but don't compromise my child's experience." The irony inherent here is one reason why change in schools is often very slow; mistakes, especially public mistakes, are frowned upon and difficult to frame.

Bug bounty is one idea from the world of startups/software that could begin to soften the culture around growth at schools—and even reframe some of the student behavior that's already happening around the edges of our technology programs. Too often in classrooms, teachers and students fail to recognize that they are playing on the same team—if the teacher provides clear and engaging instruction, students learn. If students learn, the teacher succeeds. So, for example, if a teacher is working in a learning management system like Moodle or Blackboard, both the teacher and the students would benefit from a modified "bug bounty" program wherein the teacher rewarded students who offered productive suggestions about the ways in which the interface could function more productively or with enhanced clarity. In fact, starting such a program, even informally, would allow teachers to remind students about the role they play in their own educations. Instead, many teachers signal that they do not want to be "corrected" by their students; and many students talk only to each other when they have an issue with the way in which a teacher designs, presents, or archives his or her class material. Bug bounties offer schools a productive model for creating partnerships between teachers and students. Or, to go back to what we learned from Tom Nammack, bug bounties could help educators see those things we cannot see—those things that are glaringly obvious to some of our own constituents.

LEARN TO SHARE, MIX TO DISTRIBUTE

The unspoken rule in the online world is that you will share—or, to be more precise, overshare—things that delight you or bother you, pictures and media, articles, stuff your cat or kids do, you name it. That's why sharing functions are built into much of the media we consume online . . . with the simple push of a button you can share that photo of your notes or that blog post you wrote about how to screw in a light bulb or that funny picture of your grandmother—via text or mail or Twitter or Facebook.

But . . . and that is a hard *but*, the blended leader believes in tidiness, especially in the information ecosystems where most of us work. He or she doesn't believe in sharing for the sake of sharing (or just because sharing is so simple to accomplish). He or she would never want to create digital clutter. Instead, the blended leader shares professionally for the sake of learning—sometimes to spur the learning of others, and sometimes to solidify his or her own understanding.

So there is a step—yes, another design pause like the one we saw in Belief 2—where the blended leader takes the time to shape something before sharing it. This shaping could be something simple (slapping a contextualizing caption on a photo) or much more complex (organizing and annotating a series of documents in a workflow). Such sharing celebrates—and extends—the rejection of insularity documented earlier. Also, it allows blended leaders to credit—that is, cite—the people from whom they asked for, and received, help. Finally, such sharing expresses an important idea about power: It should not be hoarded.

We have all heard the expression "Knowledge is power" because in many arenas, it's just plain true. The cliché is a cliché for a reason. If you're negotiating with a car dealer who knows a lot more than you do, he has the power. If you do your own research on the car you want to buy and get quotes from a few other dealers before walking into the dealership, then you have shifted some of the power in your direction, reducing what Hagel and Brown (2013) call "information asymmetry."

Interesting to note, in that particular example, is that the power shifts toward you because someone else made it his or her business to share knowledge with you. Someone had the same question . . . and built a website (the fruit of their inquiry) that helped you get "under the hood" of the car industry. Someone rewrote the rules of the cliché. In this case, giving away knowledge is power. Blended leaders, big and small, recognize the potential in such a counterintuitive concept.

Let's start (big) with the city of Chicago. Recently, Chicago made available a series of datasets ranging from street locations to bike routes. Using GitHub and an MIT license, they essentially told the world that they wanted any interested and informed person to "have at" the data. A report from digital.cityofchicago.org (2013) encouraged users "to improve data accuracy, combine it with other data sources, or download and use it for analysis or a new app." Modification was fine; commercial use was fine, too.

So some people would use the data on a volunteer basis, and some would use it for personal gain, but the denizens of Chicago all stand to benefit if, for example, bike paths are updated or maps are improved.

In the past, these data, like the car data mentioned earlier, were squirreled away. They was controlled by a few people who may have used them for their own interests or simply made no use of the data whatsoever. But some very savvy blended leader decided that bottling up these data was not helpful or healthy. It was not a way to actualize the potential of the data.

So what does any of this have to do with school? School leaders of all shapes and sizes squirrel away useful information, data, best practices, instructive anecdotes, and so on. More often than not, they do so inadvertently or because their systems are simply not set up to make sharing easy.

Blended leaders are interested in using technology to scale organizational learning. As a habit, they continually look at their work in real time and ask, What knowledge is valuable here and not being shared? Are we (am I) hoarding knowledge that might be useful to other leaders as they attempt to complete their work? Am I hoarding knowledge that might help others learn or approach a problem in a new way?

Can we save the institution time and/or reduce unnecessary friction by creating an archive, models, procedures that don't need to be rethought every time? Can we apply one of the most basic lessons of the software world—that is, we should not have to redo anything that is repeatable?

So, for example, a blended leader looks at email and sees a mostly closed system that could be opened slightly. He or she sees it as a system that can be gamed in some way to actualize the sharing of information or models.

In a typical email exchange, A writes to B, B writes to A, A writes to B, B writes to A, and sometimes C is copied because he or she is expected to eyeball the information but not to act on the email. If you are in the To: . . . line, you are a "doer"; if you are in the Cc: . . . line, you are an "observer."

This system works well enough to dominate much of the knowledge work that takes place in organizations (we're not saying we are happy with it, but that is a story for another chapter). Let's say a leader—Elizabeth—is working on email with one of her direct reports—Simon. Elizabeth and Simon are trying to solve an urgent problem. They bounce half a dozen emails back and forth at all hours of the day and night. Elizabeth frames the issues and asks all the right questions; Simon finds all the right answers. They solve the problem. Is Elizabeth a leader? Yes. Is she a blended leader? Kind of.

True, Elizabeth used asynchronous technology to frame issues and ask questions, but she couldn't be called a fully effective blended leader unless she took one more step—a step that requires a little bit of will and a little bit of discipline.

If we were coaching Elizabeth, we would tell her that she handled the "urgent," near-term problem well; now, to continue using Stephen Covey's terms, she has to handle what is "important" and more long term: that is, the development of other leaders through the sharing of knowledge, through the gaming of her own system to ensure that it yields the most possible benefit to the most possible people (Covey, 2004).

Let us say that Elizabeth was helping Mark, a new department chairman, to mentor a new hire for his department. She might have helped him to develop a list of people who should be involved in the mentoring process, shared a previously used Google Forms survey to aid in the evaluation of the new hire, and asked some important questions about which classes would be best for the new hire to observe in order to shore up her weaknesses and extend her strengths. Solving problems with Mark helps Mark to grow. That is the first step. Sharing the problem-solving approach used by Elizabeth and a new chairman like Mark helps other chairs, new or not, to grow. That is the extra step, the blended leader's step.

To be a truly effective blended leader, Elizabeth should find a way to repackage her online conversation, and any documents or ideas that emerged, so that other leaders can learn from the exchange. Here is where blended leadership, like all leadership, is tied to good, old-fashioned will power and self-discipline: Will Elizabeth take the time to cut and paste, contextualize, and organize documents into a file that can be referenced as often as it needs to be? Will she capture and archive the learning so that it can be shared? Will she create a checklist that explains the desired outcomes for effective mentoring? Will she make this checklist accessible to all department chairs by placing it in an area (like Moodle or Evernote) where key documents can be stored and accessed as needed? Will she become more systematic about expressing her underlying philosophy that new hires should be thought of as community members, rather than as specialists being filed into a particular silo?

Extracting and cataloguing the value of a complicated, multistep exchange sounds like a lot of work—and it is. But it is great modeling. If Elizabeth acts first, other members of her team might act next. And, in the future, they might think to copy each other—as observing learners—on similar exchanges.

EMAIL IS ABOUT KNOWLEDGE CONTROL *

EMAIL IS A MOSTLY CLOSED SYSTEM THAT CAUSES US TO HOARD INFORMATION THAT MIGHT HELP OTHERS LEARN.

* INTENTIONALLY OR NOT

In our work, as we try to continually find ways to build leadership across distance and time, it is becoming routine for people to passively share targeted information using the Cc: function. So, as Steve emails meeting agendas to a team that he oversees, he includes colleagues who oversee similar teams on different campuses. Is he cluttering their inboxes? Once a month, sure; he is adding a single email to what we all know is an overwhelming amount of email. But he notified these colleagues in advance that he would be doing this, and they know they can erase the email quickly if they don't have the time or inclination to read it. Every now and then, though, they see something on one of his agendas and they ask him a question about it. They ask him why he's doing something or how he's doing something . . . or they try a similar exercise with their own groups. This brings them closer as the leaders of their respective campuses and helps the campuses stay loosely aligned with a very limited amount of effort. It promotes the sharing of what is sometimes called "soft knowledge," which is difficult to quantify but important for the ways in which organizations function.

SHARING AND NOT SHARING

Jeff Herb, an educator, blogger, and podcaster, posted a similar idea related to passive sharing on his blog. It is worth considering in the context of this chapter. The title of his post was "Display an #edchat in your Faculty Lounge." Though many educators are aware of the numerous resources made available every day on spaces like Twitter, according to Herb there are many more educators who know very little about these conversations and are reluctant or nervous about engaging with these spaces. He suggests simply using a projector to display a live feed of #edchat-tagged tweets on the wall of a faculty room and posting a flyer that notes the times and places when the official #edchat conversations happen online. Jeff proposes five steps to creating this access (in a mere five minutes).

1. Find a clear wall in your lounge or set up a screen in a corner.
2. Set up a projector with a laptop that is connected to the internet.
3. Head to http://visibletweets.com and enter the #edchat hashtag in the space provided.
4. Choose the style you prefer—then hit View Full Screen in the bottom right corner.
5. Send out a building-wide email saying that an #edchat will be streaming in the faculty lounge and to check it out if you have a spare minute. Don't push it, those who do see it will share with their colleagues who didn't. (Herb, 2013)

Ted Parker, director of digital literacy and innovation at King, a coeducational, independent day school in Stamford, Connecticut, heard about this idea in the previous version of our book and tried it out at his school. When we spoke to Mr. Parker, he said,

> *"I'm trying to encourage a culture of independent, online professional learning. It's a disposition that has really come to define my career, but how one could possibly find the time to engage with the torrent of online information continues to mystify many of my colleagues. I liked the idea in your book about projecting #edchat in the faculty room, so I gave it a shot with #isedchat." (personal communication, April, 2014)*

When asked to reflect on the process, Mr. Parker admitted right away that "it started a few good conversations, but not much more than that." His analysis of the limitation of the project, in his teaching context, serves as a useful reminder that one size does not fit all, even when we're only talking about sharing free knowledge freely:

> *First, my timing was wrong. By the fourth quarter, most faculty are more concerned with finishing out their current projects than envisioning new ones. Second, the standard Twitter visualizers like Visible Tweets and Tweetbeam are good for displaying conversation such as what happens on #isedchat from 9–10 on Thursday evenings, but not so much the resource sharing that happens the rest of the week: tweets that share resources display a series of hashtags and URLs that, to the uninitiated, are pretty much indecipherable. As it's the resource sharing that I'm most interested in (I don't find Twitter all that great a medium for dialogue), I'm still seeking a tool that, like Flipboard, would show a preview of each tweeted link. (personal communication, April, 2014)*

BLENDED LEADING WITH DIGESTS

Here is a more complicated example. Let us say you are a member of an eleven-person team, and the team has to hire a new member. To complete the process, the team has to go through many steps together: understanding the job that needs to be filled, reviewing credentials of potential teammates, and interviewing and evaluating them. This process can easily mushroom into many emails. Imagine:

1. The leader emails the team once to invite you to a meeting. You attend.
2. The leader emails you again with the notes from the meeting. The notes contain the timeline of the hiring activities as a separate attachment.
3. The leader emails you the credentials for the three top prospects. Three more attachments.
4. The leader emails you the credentials of two more top prospects. Two more attachments.
5. Before each interview, the leader emails you additional documents. Two more attachments.
6. He emails you, too, about the location for each interview.
7. He forgets something, so he emails you again.
8. At the end, he asks for your feedback on the candidate. One more attachment.
9. Steps 5 through 8 repeat in advance of the each candidate's interview.

A good blended leader thinks continually about ways to reduce friction for others; ways to use technology—if at all—to free up people to do their best possible work. She would look at her list and see the kind of clarity that ultimately undermines itself. Roughly eight emails (per candidate) containing nine attachments sent to ten team members. Was the writer clear? Sure. Excessively so. Will the ten team members do what needs to be done to properly catalogue each email, archive each attachment, and reference the right email and attachment at the right time to ensure that the hiring process runs smoothly? Not so sure. Excessively not so sure.

So what would a good blended leader do in this situation? First, she envisions the process, in all of its complexity, before inviting her team to participate. She would take a design pause to figure out the best way to reduce friction for her team members. She would not "do things the way they have always been done"; we all know the kinds of confusion that ensue from an onslaught of even the most meticulously crafted emails. And so, in this case, perhaps she would choose a digest approach. People need the information, but they don't need the information to pop up randomly in their email stream, necessitating near extreme acts of organizational dexterity in order to make sense of it all.

We have seen this digest approach used masterfully by Tom Holt, chair of the upper school science department at Montclair Kimberley Academy. When he hires, he sends one email per candidate and uses folders in Google Docs to minimize the attentional cost for his hiring team.

Here's a typical email from Tom with details blocked out to hide some identifying details:

✕

From: Tom Holt ◀▉▉▉▉▉▉▉▉▉▉▉▶
Subject: Science Candidate tomorrow - Thursday May 7th -- AP Biology Candidate
Date: May 6, 2015 at 3:33:14 PM EDT
To: ▉▉▉▉▉▉▉▉▉▉▉▉▉▉▉▉▉▉▉▉▉▉▉▉▉▉▉▉▉▉▉

▉▉▉▉▉▉▉ will visit the Upper School on Thursday May 7th (tomorrow) and teach a demonstration lesson last period.

Please click here for a folder containing:
• Candidate Schedule
• Candidate Full File (including CV and reference letters)
• AP Biology job posting
• 7 Essential Qualities – the Science Department members will use the same/similar "STAR" questions as before in structuring their data-gathering interviews

And here is the tidy digest you see when you click the live link:

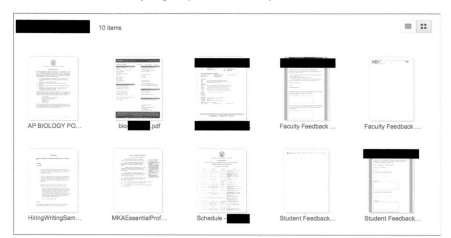

There is another layer to the story—and it is the (brutally obvious) fact that you are looking at Tom's work right now and in a position to learn from it. Tom paid nothing—by way of his own time or attention—to share this work with you. Steve was copied on the original email, and since he's charged with helping other department chairs to succeed, and hire, he saved the email and the shared folder. Next year, when Steve's school hires again, Tom Holt's mastery will guide us—and someone else will take it one step further, improve it one notch more, as we continue to try to assemble the best possible faculty. Archiving an excellent model primes excellence for further iteration.

When such work is accomplished offline and out of view, it is tough to scale. Performed online, the blended leader awake to its potential can quickly and easily capture it, contextualize it, remix it, share it, and insist on it as a future starting point. If the blended leader can achieve such a goal without burdening the master, that's all the better. The master only needs to chime in, in fact, when he decides whether or not to give permission for his/her work to be shared.

BLENDED LEADING WITH TEMPLATES

In her book *slide:ology* the peerless Nancy Duarte pushes the digest approach—or at least the thinking behind it—to one of its logical conclusion. If you are creating outward-facing presentations that represent your organization, you should be working from a previously designed, company-approved template. The digest, in this case, is not a nice-to-have but a should-have. In a chapter called "Governing with Templates," Duarte suggests:

> *When more than one person generates presentations for an organization, a well built template system is a must. Templates increase productivity, constrain exploration, and protect the investment you've made in your brand. You want your clients to have the same visceral reaction to your presentation that they have to your products, services, and ad campaigns. Unfortunately, it's usually tough for the employees building the slides to pull that off. (Duarte, 2008, p. 204)*

Read without the corporate language, this paragraph pushes us as educators and educational leaders. We, too are "ambassadors of [a] brand." In our case, a brand should represent an approach to learning, a set of values (that is, the way we approach learning, the ways in which we live the growth mindset, and so on), and our school missions.

When those approaches, values, and missions meet an outside audience, the success with which they are presented should not fall (solely) to the design skills of the presenter.

Steve and Reshan started thinking about this concept the last time they saw a large group of teachers—from the same school—present at an open house advertising their school. Every presentation they attended was homegrown. Some used PowerPoint, some used Keynote, some used Google Docs, and some used a projected MS Word document. Some used pictures, some of those pictures were cited (and some were not), some of those pictures were stock images, and some of those pictures were originals. Some presentations included student voices and some did not. Multiple fonts were used across presentations. Clearly, some teachers were very good at making presentation slides; some were much better at teaching students multivariable calculus.

After seeing the various slide presentations, Steve and Reshan had no idea about the school's mission. They understood the personal agendas of a few of the more charismatic presenters, but their overall impression of the school itself was utterly fragmented. They could have been in ten different schools that day.

SAVING OUR ASSETS

In short, sometimes a digest, archival, or template approach can be used internally to control quality. That's what we learned from the Tom Holt example. Other times, such an approach could be used to ensure that a school is presenting a united front. In the private school market, this is particularly important during open house presentations. You want families to understand the school they are considering. If they think they are choosing one school, and in reality your school is not that school, that is a lose–lose situation. It is bad for the student and bad for the school that has to attempt to realign expectations that never should have been transmitted in the first place.

Sharing one's work—whether via a simple Cc: function, a digest system, or a template system—also ensures against calamity. Though it's difficulty to contemplate, you could lose any member of your teaching faculty or administration on any given day. A blended leader understands that, in a world where professional assets are so easily captured, replicated, stored, and shared, there's no reason to lose institutional ground if you lose an important institutional player (to something tragic or simply because she leaves the school to work at another).

Returning to *The Year without Pants*, we find that Mullenweg's original blog post, announcing his plans to build his new company, talked about the importance of keeping vital and vibrant ideas—like the ones that help our schools to shine—alive:

> *Fortunately, b2/cafelog is GPL [general public license], which means that I could use the existing codebase to create a fork, integrating all the cool stuff that Michael would be working on right now if only he was around. The work would never be lost . . . if I fell off the face of the planet a year from now, whatever code I made would be free to the world, and if someone else wanted to pick it up they could. (Berkun, 2013, p. 31)*

We started this chapter by talking about the importance of humility; we can't possibly know all the answers to all the questions that school leadership will ask of us. The furthest extension of such humility is the acknowledgment that what we do learn is not only a result of our own hard work, but also a result of the luck of circumstance—that we happened to work in particular schools with particular people at particular times. We who ask countless questions have countless teachers. When we leave those teachers, and those schools, we should leave behind the best of what we found so that others can build on top of it.

MINDFUL ORGANIZING, MINDFUL ORGANIZATIONS

We all work at such a high rate of speed, racing from one task to the next. It is really not surprising that "mindfulness training" has emerged as a recent trend in leadership development.

Tony Schwartz, in a February 2013 *Harvard Business Review* blog post called "How to Be Mindful in an Unmanageable World" cites several examples of high-level executives discussing practices that they themselves use to deal with the overwhelming demands of many workplaces. Chief technology and strategy officer at Cisco Padmasere Warriuo meditates and paints. CEO of LinkedIn Jeff Weiner deliberately tries to work compassion into his leadership and management practices. Executive chairman of the Ford Motor Company Bill Ford used mindfulness and meditation to help his company overcome some of its toughest recent challenges.

These practices include putting down technology. But there's a middle ground—related directly to the kinds of sharing for which we advocate in this chapter—for the leader who would be a blended leader. A quotation from Marlys Christianson in an interview she gave to Chris Gusen for Rotman Management helps us to see how such work might look:

> *Mindful organizing is a set of organizing practices that help people not only to do things like notice problems, but also see what others are working on, so that they know how their work fits with other peoples' work. If I see that you're having a problem with something, I can help you; I can realize that what I do actually affects what you're doing. It's about being really aware of your work and other peoples' work, and how it all fits together. (Gusen, 2014).*

Christianson provides an excellent set of guidelines for the online leader who would tend to both the urgent and the important, both the problem in front of him or her and the long-term growth of the organization all around. Taking the time to understand the work of others—as Steve did with the work of Tom Holt, for example—allows you to support that work and the work of others. Asking questions about the work of others—as Reshan once did when he asked Steve about some clutter in his iCal and helped Steve adjust his calendaring practice dramatically—allows you to share, in a targeted way, resources you come across. You will be the one making sure to connect an important email to a calendar event six months from now, ensuring that your boss has access to the exact note that she needs in the exact moment she needs it.

We have been talking in this chapter (and this book) about design pauses and designing against defaults; another name for such practices is "mindfulness at work." Asking, How might I organize this team project before diving in to work with the team? Asking, Are there buckets I can establish to collect certain artifacts during an upcoming semester, so that these artifacts are easy to find and share in future semesters? We need not needlessly duplicate efforts; we need not reinvent certain wheels in every department, every month; we need not start from scratch when a star player leaves the organization; we need not needlessly frustrate one another with an endless string of email messages; we need not close off our work from one another.

Blended leadership, as a model for leadership, is, after all, largely about openness. About asking for help. About design thinking. The tools, in the end, will change (more on that later). You can take them or leave them. You can reject them as soon as you accept them. Not everyone has the time to learn new tools (in our experiences at a very tech savvy school, it's not uncommon to hear someone say, "I don't use _____ yet because I haven't had the time to play with it; I'm planning to do that this summer"). That is fine. But new technologies have led to new ways of working (that is, new ways of collaborating and new expectations for interrelatedness, access to information, input, and sharing). These new ways of working cannot be put back in the box like the digital camera that doesn't work the way you want it to.

The moves toward openness and accessibility, toward a flattening of hierarchies, cannot be put back in the box either. That leadership is tied directly to learning, and that leaders have an obligation to help others learn, cannot be refunded. In the same way that you can do a good deed without donning a superman suit, you can lead like a blended leader without using technology. The tools change; the moves do not.

BELIEFS IN PRACTICE: THINGS TO TRY #3

An Offline Thing

Next week, as you walk around your institution, attend various meetings, visit classrooms, and participate in other school routines, jot down on a piece of paper two to five challenges or inefficiencies that you observe others experiencing or that you experience with others. For each one, talk to a person whom you believe is directly affected and learn more about his or her perspective. Don't try to solve the problem right away, and don't even offer to, or promise to offer to, solve the problem. Instead, block off one hour in your calendar three weeks from now dedicated to investigating the problem(s) further. After your investigation, share the results with the person or people you originally approached.

An Online Thing

Pick one of the problems identified in the previous task. Do some Twitter searches for the related topic, and then find and follow ten people who seem to be interested in similar problems. Make a "Twitter List" of those ten people to easily see only their tweets. After two weeks, log back into Twitter and click on the list. What are they continuing to say? Has their attention moved onto other (interesting) topics? Are they still talking about the original problem?

A Blended Thing

In a face-to-face conversation, ask a couple of colleagues or team members to share with you one or two pressing questions or challenges for which they believe the expertise to resolve them does not exist within the institution. Search Twitter (or search for blogs using Google) for experts on those challenges and reach out to those experts, requesting to set up an introduction between them and your colleagues to possibly discuss further ideas related to the pressing questions or challenges. If appropriate, join in the dialogue.

Photo by Gwenael Ginder

BELIEF #4

BLENDED LEADERS CHALLENGE MEETING STRUCTURES AND CHANGE MEETING STRUCTURES

"TOO SMALL TO DO ANYTHING HARD IN"

We have all been in meetings that could have been handled through email. And we have all been part of an email chain that, because of its complexity and nuance, should have been handled in a face-to-face (F2F) meeting.

We have all had the experience of getting lost in our work, of forgetting time and restraints, of reaching what might be called a flow state—and receiving a phone call or hearing an alarm on our computer or smart phone that calls us away from that work. To a meeting.

Perhaps even more damaging, and less easily recognized, are the times we have been prevented from reaching that flow state because we are continually watching a clock or looking at our calendars or setting alarms or asking colleagues to interrupt us. Our awareness of impending meetings, and our continual need to plan for them or keep track of them, can act like an ankle bracelet keeping us under a low-grade house arrest.

Our leaders serve us best when they think about our time and our talents—how to save the former and give us the greatest opportunity to develop, exercise, and share the latter. Meetings often have the opposite effect; executed poorly, organized around the wrong set of tasks, or calling together the wrong group of colleagues at the wrong hours of the day, meetings can waste time, grind good people down, and reduce opportunities for people to share their talents.

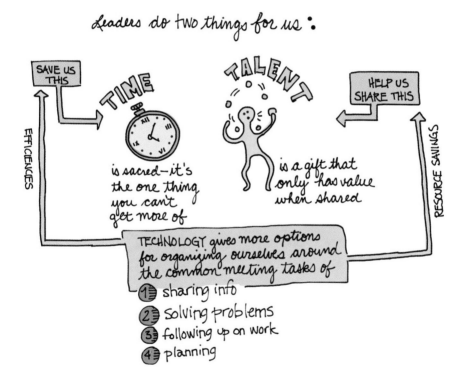

In July 2009, writing on his blog, the venture capitalist Paul Graham drew a line in the digital sand. He placed "managers" on one side and "makers" on the other, and then he described the preferred work styles of each group—how they "use time."

Managers operate out of a "traditional appointment book," slicing the day into discrete, often small, chunks. Because of their status in organizations, they have the ability to pull others into their schedules. They have the ability to slice up the work of others. Makers prefer to work in very long blocks: "units of a half a day at least." In this time, they presumably puzzle through code (if they program) or syntax (if they write) or other problems presented by their materials and their goals if they are makers of a different sort.

According to Graham, when we assemble managers and makers in the same organization, we mix two kinds of schedules. Managers relish such an arrangement. After all, they have the power to call as many meetings as they would like to have, whether those meetings deal with urgencies or more "speculative" possibilities. Not so for makers, who view meetings that break up their work as "disasters" or "like throwing an exception." In the world of programming, throwing an exception means that the program—in this case, the maker's program—jumps from the desired task to another task that now needs to be dealt with, causing the programmer—in this case, the maker—to go into debugging mode.

Graham is a careful thinker, and listening to him carefully pays dividends. What is wrong with breaking up a maker's day, with changing its expected course?

Segmenting a maker's day breaks it into pieces "too small to do anything hard in." Graham's point? Meetings are often focused on work that is not hard or valuable. Graham's implication? Certain sorts of organizationally acceptable collaborative practices aren't producing anything truly great because they don't establish the conditions for people to tackle truly hard projects. They are poorly designed, and we show up to them out of habit or because we have to.

In 2009, Morton T. Hansen was bringing fifteen years of research to fruition to help us understand the impact of such a default setting. In his book, *Collaboration: How Leaders Avoid the Traps, Create Unity, and Reap Big Results*, he makes a point that cuts against a truism that many of us have simply accepted: Collaboration is good for us. Not always, Hansen says. "Bad collaboration," he writes early in his book, "is worse than no collaboration. People scuttle from meeting to meeting to coordinate work and share ideas, but far too little gets done" (Hansen, 2009, p. 1). And he goes further: "Poor collaboration is a disease afflicting even the best companies" (p. 1).

We can move pretty easily from Graham's experience-based observations and Hansen's research-based conclusions to the world of school, where managers and makers collaborate each and every day in predictable, meeting-driven ways. We meet with our classes, our extracurricular teams, and as grade-level or department teams; we meet as committees and leadership teams; we meet as full faculties and schools; we meet "on the fly" and "on the calendar," ad hoc and in standing appointments. Sometimes these collaborative efforts lead to amazing performances—things we could not have done on our own. We have all seen amazing things happen on sports fields and stages or with curriculum and program, and these things happen as a result of repetitive, productive meetings. But sometimes, the results are not so great—we drag ourselves to meetings that lead only to a state we refer to as "meetingocrity," or mediocrity by meetings, pulling us away from other, more meaningful work.

WHAT TO DO ABOUT MEETINGOCRITY?

Graham (2009) doesn't offer concrete suggestions in his blog post . . . but then again, it is just a blog post. He expects the two sides, managers and makers, to recognize one another, be aware of one another, and try to respect one another. Fair enough.

Hansen (2009), in contrast, promotes what he calls "disciplined collaboration" or "the leadership practice of properly assessing when to collaborate (and when not to) and instilling in people both the willingness and the ability to collaborate when required" (p. 15).

Knowing when to collaborate (and when not to) is a great achievement for any leader in our schools. We tell every leader we work with that it is okay to cancel a scheduled meeting if you don't feel that you truly need it. In *Meeting Wise: Making the Most of Collaborative Time for Educators,* Kathryn Parker Boudett and Elizabeth A. City offer a simple litmus test to help you make such decisions: "If you can't tell a compelling story that explains why spending precious time convening a group of adults on a particular issue will ultimately serve learning and teaching, don't meet" (Boudett & City, 2014, p. 17).

That is a very helpful suggestion, bold even, and the book that follows it offers some highly practical and technical advice to promote effective meetings in schools. In our book, though, we are trying to take seriously the promise of blending leadership, and as a result, we are itching for more; we are interested in exploring ways that a blended approach can help us reconsider meetings altogether. Blended thinking, after all, allows us to design against the default. It is a set of "what if" questions, really. What if we did not do X at the same time we always do X? What if we moved Y into a different place or invited different people to the table? What if there were no table? What if we ran Z through a new program? More concretely, what kind of learning and doing (L&D), for teachers and students, could take place in schools if we didn't limit L&D to the block of time traditionally set aside for it and to the four walls into which it is usually crammed? What if we reimagined meetings and the collaborative practices they delimit?

As is our typical mode, we are taking at least some of our cues from the world of software developers, startups, and programmers. When successful, these groups have been relentlessly collaborative and unbelievably productive, in spite of the fact that they are sometimes made up of people who have reputations for not working well with others. When successful, these groups have solved incredibly complex problems, and in doing so, have changed everything from our computers (obviously) to our televisions to our thermostats to our phones to our cars to our baby monitors to our books to our stores to our dishwashers to our advertising to our hospitals. Their products are compelling, groundbreaking, life changing, and, as Marc Andreessen (2011) once said, "eating the world." Why wouldn't we want some, of whatever led to that, in our schools?

The Agile Manifesto

Many of the great programmers and great startup founders work differently than the rest of us. When they started their companies, or went to work in someone else's company, they did not spin their wheels in the same ruts as everyone else. They did not look at the way their fathers and mothers worked and say, "We should organize ourselves exactly like that." They examined process instead, refusing to inherit one. They looked at the kind of work they hoped to do, took seriously the ways in which external changes can affect project management and project fulfillment, and devised guidelines within which they could function best. Luckily, they took such retooling of process so seriously that they generated manifestoes to articulate their core beliefs and craft. And they fought—and still fight—over these manifestoes.

One of the most famous artifacts from these endless scuffles is the "Manifesto for Agile Software Development," published in 2001 by self-proclaimed "organizational anarchists" Martin Fowler and Jim Highsmith, and cosigned by many others. The work of Boudett and City, referenced earlier, might help you maximize the existing work environment in your school. That is, it might help you to proceed in a practical and sane manner and work with the clay you have. But it is also worth considering the work of organizational anarchists from time to time, trading in your ordinary clay for another substance, just to see what you can build with it.

The Agile Manifesto evolves from a shared appreciation for values that any school would share: "mutual trust and respect," collaboration, a focus on people and the kinds of professional communities that are attractive to the professionals who inhabit them or could, one day, inhabit them (Fowler & Highsmith, 2001). And yet it serves as an excellent foil to the working methods, and even the mindsets, of many schools.

Where many schools cling to jargon or try to force-fit technology onto their existing programs and populations, agile practitioners admit up front that they "don't have all the answers and don't subscribe to the silver-bullet theory" (Fowler & Highsmith, 2001). That kind of clear-thinking humility—especially from such brilliant people—is important for any organization that hopes to allow its frontline workers (that is, teachers) to make decisions based on what is truly best for the clients (that is, students). It leads to an important prioritization of individuals and their interactions over processes or tools, which is also a stance that we think schools should promote, especially as related to technology integration. Too many schools start by talking about bulk purchases or the hot new gadget instead of what is best for teaching and learning.

Partially, they do this because they worship the god of planning. Syllabi and lesson plans are seemingly as old as schools, and strategic plans, though newer, abound. Agile's answer to planning is characteristically humble and aspirationally in line with reality:

> No one can argue that following a plan is a good idea—right? Well, yes and no. In the turbulent world of business and technology, scrupulously following a plan can have dire consequences, even if it's executed faithfully. However carefully a plan is crafted, it becomes dangerous if it blinds you to change. (Fowler & Highsmith, 2001)

AGILE, PANDA, SCRUM, SELF-ORGANIZING SYSTEMS ARE ALL

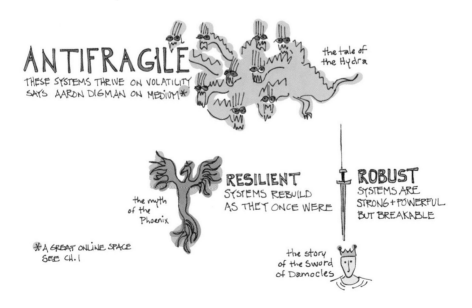

Change, for Agile practitioners, is something to be courted rather than feared, managed rather than resisted. They know—from little more than the long experience of being human—that change is a law of the universe. It happens.

Another thing that schools might learn from Agile methodology is how to take seriously one of the things they dole out most frequently: feedback. One of the keenest ironies of schools is that the adults who populate them, who supposedly love learning so much that they dedicate their working lives to it, often have trouble applying their own learning to their own daily practice. Agile methodology foregrounds this, again very human, maladaptation with a direct and penetrating statement: "Although most people agree that feedback is important, they often ignore the fact that the result of accepted feedback is change." Agile teams, though self-organizing, work with change; they change as a result of change; they trust their "ability to respond to unpredictable events more than [their] ability to plan ahead for them" (Fowler & Highsmith, 2001).

As has happened since its inception, however, the Agile methodology espoused in the Agile Manifesto is often critiqued, and we can learn, too, from such assays. Giles Bowkett, who works with Panda Strike, published a paper online on March 4, 2015. Called "Flaws in Scrum and Agile," Bowkett's memo points out the way times have changed. In it, he talks about the fact that tools like GitHub, Skype, and Hangouts had not been popularized when Agile was first codified. As a result, Agile's insistence on face-to-face communication is somewhat anachronistic. As Bowkett writes:

> Remote work requires a ton of writing, and that's one of the best things about it.
>
> How many times have you sat down to email somebody a question, and found that in the process of writing the email, the answer became obvious to you? This step is built in to the workflow of every remote team. Likewise, have you ever had to tell a co-worker the same thing twice? Technical work involves lots of tradeoffs, and people don't always remember the intricacies of every debate. But you can refer to a conversation on GitHub three years later and review every detail with perfect clarity. In a distributed company, the written word becomes much more influential than the spoken word. (Bowkett, 2015)

This takedown of Agile, truth be told, feels like what we are promoting in this book: logical and rational moves forward, in a variety of areas of organizational life (mainly in schools) based on existing tools and cultural norms that are bubbling just below the "old-school" sheen and surface.

For our purposes, though, the details of Agile methodology—and its critics—is not as important as the spirit that drives its practitioners. And the system preference is not as important as the fact that such systems were invented, fought over, spawned spinoff systems, and continue to power today's software and startup workforces. It is healthy to analyze not only the products produced by teams, but also the teaming practices and workflows that generated those products. (The next time you want to discuss homework practices, perhaps you could organize the conversation in grade levels rather than departments, or vice versa, depending on your school's typical pattern.) It is healthy to connect meetings as directly as possible to work being done on behalf of the customer or end user. (The next time you are deciding on an important school policy, consider inviting some students into the process.) It is healthy to relentlessly try to omit needless work. (Pick a process that bugs you in your school and then organize a group to reduce it by at least two steps.) It is healthy to reflect and adjust—continuously. (All good teachers do this; all good leaders of teachers should, too.) It is healthy to allow teams to self-organize, to find their own way to work, based on what they discern from their local environments and the specific problems they face. (Some schools choose the unconference method when they are addressing issues in their community; rooms are assigned based on topics; participants then join the conversation that interests them and stay only as long as they feel they can contribute.) You don't need to follow the Agile Manifesto to promote growth and change in your school, but it might not be a bad idea to have your own manifesto—to be clear about how you work together and why you work together, and to be appropriately critical of the organizational habits and default settings you haven't questioned in a while.

FACE-TO-FACE (F2F) MEETINGS

We want to take an especially critical look at F2F meetings because they cause the most disruption in people's schedules, which means the most disruption in people's ability to design their own best productivity patterns and find their best personal work rhythms. If you are going to ask people to take time out of their day to meet F2F, you should at the very least stop and ask yourself if a traditional meeting is the best use of everyone's time. Not only "Is this going to help student learning," but also "Is a F2F meeting the best way to help student learning? Is there a better way to use the talent of my team?"

Why do we meet F2F? Because we have always met F2F. How do we meet F2F? For the most part, in the same ways we have always met F2F. In a world of connected devices, these are unsatisfying answers. Blended leaders never assume that meetings have to be F2F. If they call a F2F meeting, they do so deliberately and intentionally, and to serve a very specific purpose. Technology gives us more options than ever before to solve our meeting problems.

There are two main ways to move away from F2F meetings. One is a rather idealistic rethinking of meetings; the other is a disruption of existing meeting patterns.

Rethinking the Ideal

If totally free from the typical meeting conventions, blended leaders only arrange a meeting if they have thought first about the intended outcome of the meeting and determined that they cannot arrive at that intended outcome on their own. This idea doesn't seem revolutionary—until you think about the number of meetings you attend that don't fit one or both of its criteria.

Having arrived at the conclusion that a meeting is necessary, blended leaders then define the tasks needed to reach the intended outcome. They answer the questions, what will we need to do to reach the desired outcome, and how will we do what we need to do?

Next, they think about the available talents of the people in their community and in their extended network. As has been discussed elsewhere in this book, a blended leader might use his or her extended network to solve a problem rather than turning to a more established team within his or her school. So blended leaders planning a meeting would ask themselves, who can help me solve this problem? Who needs to be part of this problem-solving (or problem-framing) process? What team should I build around this issue? These questions embody the idea put forward in Johansen's *Leaders Make the Future*: "The best leaders will get extremely skilled in choosing which medium—including in-person meetings—is good for what" (Johansen, 2012, p. 12).

We have found that it helps to think of your meeting time as a circle. Working within the circle, with familiar associates, can be beneficial in that it gives you continuous access to the institutional memory of the group. Also, the group shares tacit knowledge, which allows for shorthand when time is tight. But what happens if you remove part of that circle? Suddenly, the rest of the world can enter your meeting space. The meeting continues, with the agenda steering it, but ambient participants can influence the outcome.

If you like this idea, remember one simple fact: Every time a computer is open during a meeting and connected to the Internet, the close-knit meeting circle is broken. This can lead to distraction—as it often does, especially if the meeting is not compelling—or to the inclusion of specialists from anywhere in the world. You can bring in a relevant article or video; you can bring in a participant who can offer a fresh set of eyes and ears to help you gain a new perspective on your problem; you can record parts of your meeting, transcribe them through a transcription service like Rev, and share them with other groups working on a similar problem. Once you get used to breaking the circle, your meetings can begin to move from calm, dry, carefully conducted symphony performances to the focused serendipity of a rendition of John Cage's 4'33". If you ask the right questions while planning your meeting, and then lift the constraints associated with most meetings, you might surprise yourself and others—you might allow noise to reveal its music, passive audience members to become musicians, and the music of your organization to go where it wants to go.

Disrupting the Real

But not every meeting can be set only after someone determines one is necessary, especially in schools. Because we often work backward from a schedule of meetings, we therefore walk backward into those meetings, wondering what, if anything, there is to do.

Because of the nature of school calendars, meetings often need to be scheduled months in advance. In fact, if you do not schedule your meetings months in advance, you may not be able to schedule a meeting when you need one. So, we schedule meetings just in case we need them, and then we end up using them, even if we don't. Also, many of these prescheduled meetings are based on the assumption that teams in schools need to meet on a repetitive basis. Typical teams include grade levels, departments, student support services, administration, committees, and faculties.

A blended leader inherits such meetings, just like everybody else. But a blended leader enters his or her long march of meetings with the intent of disrupting at least a few of them in the name of time and talent.

You can begin disrupting a long march of meetings by asking questions of yourself and others. In fact, you should create a discipline around asking such questions each and every time you see a meeting approaching in your calendar.

Do we need to meet F2F? Is there a way we could accomplish the same tasks without being in the same room at the same time? Is there a way, in fact, that not meeting in the traditional way could actually enhance the outcome of the "meeting"?

The blended leader is committed to figuring out the best way to access people's best work at a time in their days when they are most capable of producing that work. We all have ideal work rhythms; we all have ideal work times. The interconnectedness of our computing devices means that meetings can happen asynchronously, matching up with those rhythms and times, aligning talents with tasks.

If Joe is a morning person, he can contribute to a shared document at 5 a.m. If Kim has parenting duties that occupy her mornings and her early evenings, she can contribute in the late evening.

If Benedict wants to share information with a group, he might simply email that information to the group.

If Sonya wants to both share information and seek input on it, she could create a Google Doc, share it with her team, and ask people to add comments in the margins.

If a discussion is not progressing as it should in a F2F meeting, why not cut off the meeting and ask people to contribute to the discussion over the next week in a wiki-style space? Or why not start the conversation there, a week before the F2F meeting?

Building a presentation with a group? Meet F2F quickly to launch the parameters of the project, then launch a Google Presentation or a Prezi presentation and ask people to contribute slides.

Facing a time-sensitive situation and having trouble getting all the key players in a room? Consider using Google Hangouts or asking someone to phone in or Skype in. You could bring in a special guest or consultant the same way.

Different modes of communication or meeting have different affordances and limitations depending on the context and purpose of that communication or meeting. A F2F meeting in the same physical space could be an organized group or committee, or it could be an informal conversation between colleagues in the hallway. A F2F meeting can also occur with individuals in different physical spaces using video-conferencing tools such as Google Hangouts. Voice meetings can happen with telephone conference calls or VoIP (Voice over IP) conversations using Skype. Synchronous text meetings can take place in a live Google Doc, through a Twitter exchange, or in iChat. Asynchronous text meetings can take place in a Google Doc or simply over email.

None of these modes is intrinsically good or bad. Instead it is important to understand what is gained and what is missing from each mode when making a decision about what type of communication structure to engage or what kind of meeting to organize. For example, a meeting can take place with a smaller subgroup of a larger committee or department, or a meeting can be run without requiring all members to be in the same space (some can participate virtually, while others can be sitting in the room).

It is also important to return to the fundamental rationale for working in teams to begin with: to achieve goals that cannot be achieved by a single person working in isolation.

When Steve and Reshan first started using technology to enhance teaching and learning in schools (more than a decade ago), one of the first truisms to pick up steam was that using an electronic message board could help quieter students to participate in your classroom discussions. Steve and Reshan saw the efficacy of this insight early and often—and, these days, it is one of the main reasons they introduce a tool like Edmodo into their classes. A well-run classroom discussion is a great way to challenge students, air and stretch ideas, and even collect formative assessment data. But some students are simply more comfortable—and productive—when they are invited to show their knowledge and skills in a different mode.

If you are responsible for surfacing talent on a team, for ensuring that the team gives all it can, changing up the communication channel can do more than simply free up people to work in ways that they want to; it can help them reveal aspects of themselves, and their abilities, that they might not be able to show in a more traditional, F2F meeting–driven venue. What happens when the person who talks too much in F2F meetings is forced to type his or her thoughts into a comment box instead? What happens to the person who talks too little? What happens to interruption patterns?

A relevant platform that has been making a lot of positive noise in business, and that is just starting to inch into schools, is called Slack. Many people are cheering for it because it is proving to reduce dependency on email and on the need to hold meetings. Who wouldn't love such a product? Slack recently closed a $160 million round of funding, valuing the company at $2.6 billion.

Photo courtesy of Slack

Slack describes itself as "a platform for team communication: everything in one place, instantly searchable, available wherever you go." In its HTML header, it includes the phrase "Be less busy." It is a combination of instant messaging, Twitter-style chat, and Evernote (because of the archival and searchable nature of the content).

Reshan was first introduced to Slack by his Explain Everything colleagues in the Poland office. They were using it to communicate across departments but also to communicate among the whole staff. Significant decisions at Explain Everything about the design of the app, the direction of the business, and more have all been mediated by Slack, with participants working in different time zones and countries. Though it is another platform—and thus another app, another login, another thing to check, and another habit to build—it somehow balances simplicity on the surface with incredible depth and reliability beneath. It also has a terrific search function.

A few months later, Reshan joined another organization that also was using Slack as its communication platform. The coworking space AlleyNYC uses Slack to make announcements to the three hundred–plus companies using their space, but individuals also use it as an opportunity to share ideas and ask questions. At AlleyNYC, Slack serves as a virtual network within a physical network. For example, Reshan posted the CV of someone interested in a summer internship to the #development channel and within hours five companies were interested in talking to the student who had asked him for this favor.

After a short time, and seeing two organizations that are vital to him using the tool, Reshan decided to give it a try for a small venture he ran with nine high school seniors (Startup 101, first mentioned in Belief 2). Knowing that the members would be working on different projects, and possibly working in different places, this platform would provide a real-time connection to bridge distance. It would, in fact, allow Startup 101 to function in a much—much!—different way than any other high school academic experience that these nine students had ever had. They could work on the project, and work with one another, whether they chose to come to the physical "classroom" space or not. Some days, Reshan would insist on F2F meetings, though most days the students would decide where to work. Slack made this flexibility possible. In addition, Slack allowed Reshan to open up the Startup 101 experience to others; he invited outside mentors and advisors to join in the conversation.

Students were invited to join Slack on the first day of the program. Other than a quick overview of channels versus messages, Reshan offered very little guidance. Once the students got comfortable with the medium, which took about one day, they started using it often and always. At first they thought they had to use the @channel syntax in order to send a message, so on day one there were a lot of notifications about every comment, but they soon realized that such a command was needed only to force a notification to their peers' devices. By the second day they realized it was not necessary except for important alerts, which they self-categorized. They contributed twelve communications in the first day, and this daily volume increased by a factor of 3 by the end of the week. A quick glance at the archives shows that they contributed an average of 150 communications per week. They introduced shared Dropbox and Google Drive folders, asked for feedback on visual designs and business plans, and decided where and what time to eat lunch. As the overseer of the project, Reshan could check in on the Slack channels from anywhere to have a sense of what the students were working on, what questions they had, and where they might be at any time. On Slack the team handled small, logistical things like field excursion travel plans, but they also worked on, and worked out, big, mission-critical problems. An example of the latter is how they decided what tool to use to build their constituent survey, how to analyze and share the results, and how to make use of their resulting insights during their final pitch to a group of potential investors.

Slack allows us to make a point that, for those who are willing to participate in a new way and take responsibility for their learning and communication in a new environment, meeting structures need not remain static. Inside Slack you can keep track of all communications, which is really what a meeting is. You can link to Google Docs when you want to build larger thinking spaces. You can generate new topics, new content areas. And the truly beautiful thing is that anyone within the space can launch these tasks, so the agenda is not controlled by one person; it is really controlled by the flow of work itself and by the needs of the team. Thus, the group sets the norms and lets the norms evolve. There is no fixed system for moving tasks or communicating. The group dictates what works for them through their use. The leader helps them see what is working for them and what is not working. And it all becomes searchable.

Trello is another tool that is challenging our meeting, collaboration, and productivity habits. It describes itself as "the easy, free, flexible, and visual way to manage your projects and organize anything." And it is another tool that came into Reshan's (and thereafter Steve's) life because of his work with Explain Everything, where the team uses it to set goals and monitor progress of tasks. It has guided them through development challenges, artwork design, and the creation of marketing materials.

When learning about the second edition of their initial book prototype, Reshan and Steve decided to use Trello to keep track of all the moving parts within Google Docs. Email remained sufficient for originating tasks. But given other systems that both Reshan and Steve maintain for their personal organization (for example, inbox zero and iCal), and the amount of condensed work and external deadlines, we needed something less linear and, more important, less intrusive to other, existing systems.

JILLIAN JONES ON SLACK

One of the students in the group, Jillian Jones, currently a freshman in the University of Pennsylvania's Wharton School of Business, offers a user's eye view of how Slack helped her team to succeed in ways that would have been difficult without it.

My first experience with Slack was on the first day of my senior project, Startup 101. While it was a foreign program to me, it almost immediately made sense.

Slack helped our team stay organized and continue to communicate with each other, even when not together. By using channels, we were able to keep our business, design, and marketing tasks separate; also it allowed us to include anyone who was interested in helping complete the tasks. This was especially true for the art and design team, where they were able to quickly share their updated mockups for the app and the logo design. Using any other mainstream forms of communication would have been very difficult or even impossible because of the size, type, and frequency of the files that they were sending out to the rest of the members in Startup 101.

When using Slack, the Startup 101 team was constantly sharing documents, new and updated versions, that would have been too overwhelming had we used email. Setting up several group chats for each component of the project would have been confusing and annoying, but Slack gave us the capabilities to consolidate into one application where everyone could stay-up-to date with daily operations, but also have the ability to focus just on the communications that are tied to their responsibilities.

I believe that Slack kept our team on task, where without Slack, we would have struggled to remain so. One aspect of our senior project that we could all agree on was that there was no one telling us what to do like in high school. We needed to be able to recognize the things we needed to do and fix our problems ourselves. Without Slack, we would not have been able to see our tasks as clearly. Through Slack, we stayed a cohesive group that could easily identify our strengths and weaknesses and immediately improve upon them.

The great thing about Slack is that the teams just have to be willing to use the app in order for it to become useful. However, I do believe that the teams have to recognize and be motivated to become more efficient in their communication. Without this ability, I do not think that teams will be using the application most effectively.

Desktop computer operating systems have files and folders. Evernote uses notes and notebooks. Trello uses boards and cards. Similar to using a sticky note board or cork board, you have boards that you can imagine are on a wall, and then cards that have specific categories or tasks within a category. Text and attachments can be added to a card, and a labeling system allows you to color code the progress or status of an item.

Photo courtesy of Trello: Adam Simms

Trello integrates with Slack, so that if a task is completed or updated in Trello, an announcement can be sent in Slack to the relevant individuals or to a specific channel.

Let us compare this functionality to the ideal scenario after a F2F meeting. After a long meeting, the leader generally consolidates and distributes follow-up actions in a timely fashion. But, in schools, where leaders are surrounded by hundreds of fellow humans who need their attention, they can't always process their notes immediately after meetings. Things come up. Sometimes it is easier to head home and think, "I'll get to those notes later." Sometimes days pass; sometimes the notes remain mere scrawls on a pad or in a program. So, the possibility of automating part of this responsibility by connecting Trello, or some similar application, to Slack, or some similar application, is incredibly enticing. Doing so would take work off the leader's plate; more important, it would all but guarantee that the leader's team would receive continual, reliable updates on their shared work-in-progress.

Preparation

We are mentioning Slack and Trello not because we think you should rush out and use them (though they are pretty amazing and definitely worth considering, especially for some of your forward-thinking teams). We hold them up as examples of how the world of work could change if you let it. We hold them up to remind you that there are other ways to organize teams. The technology is getting better every day, and students who experience this technology (maybe because they work with someone like Reshan when they are eighteen) could be applying for jobs at your school in a few short years. Will you be ready for them? Will your school be an enticing place of employment for them?

Slack and Trello offer opportunities for anyone, in any industry, looking to shake up their collaborative practices and potentially reduce the number of F2F meetings that are necessary in any given work cycle.

But you cannot simply drop a new technology onto a faculty or a team and expect that it will replace the need to meet F2F. Arriving at a point of reduced F2F meetings (some would call this nirvana) takes consideration and skill. You can only give people control of their time when they are willing to dive into something that is structured and designed to meet their needs.

If you want to mess productively with sacred meeting structures, you have to prepare the people on your team. Though many people complain when they have to attend F2F meetings, they may not be entirely comfortable leaving them behind, or may be less comfortable moving to an unfamiliar online environment.

Think about the meetings you attend (and don't run) on a regular basis. You probably wander in near the start of the meeting. Maybe you have done some thinking in advance; maybe you have not. You grab a snack if your leader has provided one. You socialize. You have a set role to play; even the jokes in some meetings will wander down well-worn and comfortable pathways. You look around the room at the other participants and bask in the warm glow of validation—you, too, have a seat at the table. In fact, because it is a table, there are only so many seats. That scarcity is attractive; it confers status. Though you might make better use of your time elsewhere, you are certainly not uncomfortable. When the leader arrives, he or she produces an agenda. He or she gives a report or asks for a report. You drift in and out of focus. Eat another cookie. The coffee is warm. When the spirit moves you, you ask a question. Sometimes someone asks you a question. Sometimes you vote. You might leave with a task or maybe just a vague understanding of what transpired. On the way out, you roll your eyes at a friend, who rolls his eyes back at you. All part of the production.

Okay, so maybe some of that prior paragraph is an exaggeration. But if you want to move away from F2F meetings, even just a few times a year, you have to move against substantial inertia, substantial institutional memory, and substantial beliefs of "That's the way we've always done things."

Also, you may be asking people to do more than they have usually done. It is worth noting, and remembering, that in an online meeting, responsibility shifts from the person who called the meeting to the people participating in the meeting. F2F, the meeting is dropped on people, and often, they tolerate it until they can slide out from under it. Move away from that model to something more digital and the meeting is then built, keystroke by keystroke and moment by moment, by the participants.

So you have to prepare people for the shift in responsibility, and the amped-up participation requirement, that happens when you move a meeting online. As Jillian, Reshan's student, said earlier, "Teams have to recognize and be motivated to become more efficient in their communication. Without this ability, I do not think that teams will be using the application most effectively."

If you plan to experiment with alternative meeting formats, first call your team together (yes, F2F) and explain what you will try and why you will try it. Then, explain to them, or even show them, what they will have to do to participate. You have to invest some time up front before an online option can become a habit.

And you have to acknowledge, up front, that your first—and maybe your second and third—online meeting might go awry. Explain that possibility to people; tell them that you are committed to moving some of your meetings online out of respect for their time and talent, and that you want them to become adept at participating in such meetings so that such meetings become another tool for the team to rely on as they seek to do meaningful work together (remember your Agile methodology—individuals and interactions are more important than processes and tools. The latter can, does, and should change as needed in Agile organizations).

Explain, too, that you expect your team members to participate vigorously, to be as curious and committed and engaged as ever. If, for example, you replace a meeting with an email and a request for feedback, it's not okay for someone to fail to read the email. And it is not okay for someone to merely glance at the email. Replacing a F2F meeting with an online meeting grants people autonomy to do the work at a time that suits them, not to avoid the work altogether. There is a deep irony here: that we sometimes waste the most attentive and responsible people's time in F2F meetings because we cannot count on the least attentive and least responsible people to read emails.

Next, be sure people know what they need to know about the technology. You might have to invest some time on training. In schools, we are often so busy that we cannot even think about upfront costs to make something easier six months from now. A blended leader invests early to save—again and again—late.

Finally, do not go overboard; do not replace all your F2F meetings all at once. People can feel disconnected if they do not sit in the same room with their teams. There is a social element that is lost when you take that away. Like many transitional phases, and like blended leadership itself, a hybrid of old and new probably works best. If you can cut short some of your F2F meetings by digitally lengthening them, you will serve people's needs (for time and balance) as well as their talents (they do not have to perform on the spot always), and you will allow work to grow and iterate and mature for as long as possible.

THE DANCE OF THE BLENDED LEADER

Blended leadership undergirds, makes possible, change in practice. That's the simplest way to put it. In this chapter, we looked at meeting practice in an attempt to goad you into attempting some meeting format experiments. If nothing else, blended leadership offers you a set of questions, a set of approaches, a way of rethinking your work and the way you join others in completing that work. Perhaps more important, it gives you a language for explaining your process (and your experiments with process) to others.

In our "introduction" we cited the work of Professor Charles R. Graham, and it becomes instructive, again, as we begin to close out our thinking on meetings. According to Professor Graham, one of the reasons teachers choose blended instruction is "increased access/flexibility" (Graham, 2006). Much of what we have discussed in this chapter is an attempt to gain one or the other of those benefits. Beyond mere conveniences, though, blended instruction—which we are not differentiating from blended leadership right now—makes available "programs that would not be possible if students were not able to have a majority of their learning experiences at a distance from instructors and/or other students . . . " (Graham, 2006, p. 9).When you begin to think of blended possibilities for your meetings, you begin to realize that you can bring almost any kind of learning, inspiration, or partner—in the world!—into your meeting.

Also, you can continue to work as your core team members embark on their own exciting professional journeys. Over the years, Reshan and Steve have enjoyed this kind of professional collaboration. Sometimes we have met in our offices; sometimes we have met in Ramen noodle shops; sometimes we have met on phones; sometimes we have met via screens; and one time we met—with an entire conference room full of people in Boston—by connecting Steve's phone to the mic jack, allowing Reshan to join and contribute from

Chicago. All these meetings mix together in our minds, and none was any better or worse because of the mode in which we made them happen; we stayed committed to our partnership, enjoyed it, and our work rolled on . . . and on . . . and into this book, regardless of time and circumstance.

A last pitch needs to be made for quality of life—the quality of life made possible by blended practice. Graham notes that "learner flexibility and convenience is also of growing importance as more mature learners with outside commitments (such as work and family) seek additional education" (Graham, 2006, p. 9). Once we have a job, we are all mature learners with outside commitments. It doesn't matter if those commitments are growing families, aging parents, or sick pets. Granted, people have been juggling work and life for years, but if technology makes new kinds of engagement possible, reducing stress, then the only thing binding us to old, legacy style meetings is . . . us.

Interestingly, when Reshan added a "dial-in" option for one of his committees that met after school, a few people exercised the option almost every time, hustling home to meet their kids and then connect to the meeting via Google Hangouts. But other meeting members said they greatly preferred to be present in the room. They appreciated the option, gave their full blessing to those who used it, but felt more comfortable, more productive, and less anxious being in a physical room with their colleagues.

So that's the rub, and also the opportunity to be the best blended leader you can be. Different people will have different preferences. One colleague's freedom is another colleague's constraint, and vice versa. Ultimately, going through this thinking and questioning process is the blessing of being blended; it forces a back-and-forth, a tug-of-war, that either dismantles or enshrines the default setting. Simply asking the questions—"Should we meet face to face or not? Will an online meeting actually enhance the work we are doing?"—should improve your F2F meetings, as well as inform your decision about whether or not to call one. You should have a high standard for calling one, for taking key players from your school out of the mix of school, away from their students or their planning, away from their grading. Continue to call F2F meetings, sure. Just don't take them for granted. Just don't forget you are making a tradeoff. And make sure you're trading everyone's time and attention for something truly worthwhile.

The dance of the blended leader is, just that, a dance. It doesn't, and shouldn't, end. We've given you a few "lines in the sand" in this chapter (and we're about to offer one more). The blended leader expresses these lines in his or her practice. First, there was Graham's (2009) separation of managers and makers. It's good to know about that line and to honor it when possible. Next, we gave you Boudett and City's (2014) line, helping you know when to cancel meetings or improve them. Finally, we give you our own line. When you call people together, at a certain time and to a certain room, you should do something with those people, during that time, and in that room that can only happen at, and because of, that specific gathering. It should be special, different, truly one-of-a-kind work. Such work requires you to be alive to the possibilities in each person, and to do your best to bring forth those possibilities.

We know of no better way to end this chapter than to share some thinking from Curt Lieneck, director of technology at the University of Chicago Lab Schools, who once joined us virtually to say to following:

> *What does school start to look like when we intentionally create educative experiences that can only happen there? What can and should we do to wring the most value from all the trouble we take to assemble a very particular set of people in the same place at the same time? How can we think more broadly and purposefully about how we use space, time, people and programs to create unique experiences that are consistently greater than the sum of their component parts?*
>
> *I once had the pleasure of attending a premier collegiate crew regatta while vacationing in California. The raw power these athletes could generate with such lean physiques was stunning. Having been an athlete in my younger days, I understood something about how much pain must accompany this level of extreme performance, so I asked one of the athletes why he put himself through all the agony it takes to excel in the sport. He said, "When we do this right, and we are all rowing as one, the boat actually leaves the water and we are gliding above its surface. When that happens, we all feel it, and it's euphoric. We work this hard so all of us can get that feeling whenever we row. It doesn't always happen, but we always try."*
>
> *This is how I dream a school should be. The crew racer must be on the water, in a boat, with other teammates and a coxswain to make this happen. For him or her, it cannot happen anywhere else. All the training, stretching, weight lifting, strategy sessions, and practicing may happen somewhere else, at some other time, but when the race is on, there is only the boat, the water, and each other. Creating experiences that simply cannot happen anywhere else is the key to unlocking the magic in a school.*

If you are going to be together in school, be together. Because, when you do that well, you do something special and you build something truly sui generis. You do something that can't be shipped over Wifi; something that cannot unfold asynchronously; something that will not tolerate multitasking, partial attention, headphones, screens, or the *bleep, bloop, blop* of digital reminders. Some things can and should flow through digital channels; other things never should. That is why we—who go to school—go to school.

BELIEFS IN PRACTICE:
THINGS TO TRY #4

An Offline Thing

For your next one-on-one meeting, arrange to have a walking meeting outside (assuming both participants are able to be mobile and the weather is cooperative). Before you head out, the other participant and you should jot down on a piece of paper all the things you mean to discuss. Plan to carry this paper with you. Set a destination that is about 10 minutes away and begin walking. If you have time once you reach the destination, stop there and find a place to sit or stand before heading back. What was different about this experience than a typical office meeting? Were you facing each other the whole time? Or walking side by side toward a similar destination? What were the limitations?

An Online Thing

Before the next meeting of a committee you lead (or, conversely, you can propose this idea to the leader of the committee), instruct all members to set up Google Plus accounts. For those that are new (or old) to social media, encourage them to look up the privacy settings available for the account so they know what part of their presence in the space is public or private. Schedule a Google Hangout inviting only the committee members. Instruct all members to join the meeting from wherever they prefer—their home, their office, a classroom (not while driving, though). Make yourself available via phone and email 15 minutes before the start of the meeting to assist with any technical challenges, and also allocate the first 5–10 minutes of the meeting to helping all members become more comfortable with the space. Then, run the meeting. At the end of the meeting, ask members about what they felt was lost and gained by conducting a real-time meeting in this manner.

A Blended Thing

For the next group meeting you lead, provide three options for how people can participate: (1) Attend in person in real time. Show up in the meeting room at the start of the meeting and leave at the end of the meeting. (2) Attend virtually in real time via video conference. Projected on a screen in the room, virtual participants can join via Skype or Google Hangout. (3) Participate asynchronously. As the leader, you must provide an agenda and specific questions at least 48 hours in advance of the meeting within a Google Doc. Asynchronous participants are responsible for posting their responses and follow-up questions within the document before the start of the real-time meeting (no excuses—they are either there in real time or have contributed in advance of the meeting). During the meeting, all real-time participants (virtual and in-person) should take notes within a Google Doc. After the meeting, asynchronous participants are expected to read the notes and add final comments and thoughts within 24 hours of the end of the real-time meeting. You, the leader, should then go through the notes, summarizing and organizing the document, and send the document as a PDF attachment in an email to all participants, with any action items and assignees listed in the body of the email.

Photo by Magnus Lindvall

BLENDED LEADERS ARTICULATE A MISSION AND ADVANCE A MISSION

IF A MISSION FALLS IN THE WOODS

On any given day, a school leader might be greeted, by chance or by design, by an extraordinary array of tasks. As mentioned earlier in this book, school leaders sometimes ensure that classrooms have enough trash receptacles. A few minutes later, these same leaders might facilitate a workshop on teaching strategies or help a group consider a major shift in curriculum or discuss an incident with an angry parent or ensure that a booklist is appropriately multicultural. These examples, and the dozens of others we could have included, highlight the everything-but-the-kitchen-sink nature of school leadership.

But if we were to boil down most school leaders' job descriptions, they reduce to a similar sauce. Really. Effective school leaders align activity in their area with the school's mission, and they are successful to the extent that their area of school life reflects every area of school life (that is, the mission). For example, if you are running an extracurricular club or an after school sports team or leading a department or a division, then your goal is to make that club/team/department/division reflect the mission of the school.

The word "*reflects*," of course, is sneaky, and we mean it that way. There is alignment—making sure decisions and behaviors hedge closely to the language of the mission—and then there is the reflection of that alignment—making sure to manifest mission-specific work or activity. The former suggests getting things done; the latter suggests demonstrating what got done. The subtle (sneaky) difference between the two modes arises naturally from the kinds of educational environments in which we currently teach, learn, and lead.

Over the past decade, schools have been increasingly unbundled. Much of what used to take place mainly in school buildings and classrooms now takes place, at least in part, virtually anywhere. Students can learn in a classroom in your school or they can travel abroad. They can learn from you face to face or they can learn from you screen to face. That is why we're here together—writing this book, reading this book. As schools shift, the story of school mission shifts too. Mission is executed (that is, is aligned to behavior) less and less behind closed doors because there are fewer closed doors available to educational enterprises. It is possible to see the lesson plan, the test, the video, the student work, the archive of letters from the principal, the photograph, the tweet, the course list, sometimes the grades . . . from the comfort of one's home, car, office, train, bed, or hotel. School gets done in more places than it used to, which means that school is demonstrated for more audiences than it used to be. We can ask which comes first in the twenty-first century: alignment to mission or demonstration of mission?

It is a typical blended conundrum with a typical blended answer—both. And we are not going to tell you what should get done in your school or what your school should stand for, other than to say that schools should stand for something—an approach to learning, a set of traditions that promote excellence, a religious affiliation, a set of beliefs. But in our world of technological bullhorns, where everyone has equal access to communication platforms and tools, silence about one's mission is not an option. In fact, even living out one's mission quietly in the corner of a school is not enough. You have to live it and show it. In the schools we have today, if a mission falls in the woods and no one is around, it does not make a sound. And no constituent is served by such silence—not the student who should derive motivation and focus from the school's mission, not the parent who should partner with the school to support the school's mission, not the teacher who should inspire students to reach for the school's mission, not the alumni who should proudly support the school's future.

Blended leaders understand the mission-critical nature of properly broadcasting one's mission, and they are the ones who ask, and live, the newest mission-related questions that occur when the digital presses in on the nondigital.

- What aspect of the lived school mission should be visible online? Should such Web content be visible internally, externally, or both?
- What parts of school life should not be visible? What parts of school should be private for the teacher and/or the student?
- Should you invest in demonstrating your school's mission in action as it unfolds—hour by hour—or should every media image pass through a central communications office?
- Should you invest in producing "long-tail" content that could be browsed or drilled into by niche audiences trying to connect to your school or understand it better?
- How does any of this activity around mission actually promote and stimulate student learning?

We can begin to answer these questions by first looking at examples of digital strategies outside of education and then returning to examples from the world of education. The story of mission is being rewritten in some unlikely places and some increasingly lively ways.

BETWEEN TWO FERNS AND WTF

The *Economist* is as distinguished and trusted a newspaper as many of us are likely to see in our lifetimes. Read by presidents and aspirants, business leaders and business students, it is 171 years young. In fact, many people who subscribe to it (in our experience) see it as a near-solemn part of their weekly routine. It piles up on the nightstand quickly, and if you fall behind in reading it, you feel like you're letting someone down.

On November 6, 2014, forming and maintaining a relationship with the newspaper's content became a bit easier. On that day, the *Economist* Espresso was launched. The newspaper's website calls it "a new morning briefing from the editors of the *Economist*." The website also announces the fact that this briefing will be "delivered to your smartphone or inbox before breakfast" and will help you make sense of "the global agenda in the coming day" ("Get Help with Economist Espresso," 2014).

Coming from the *Economist*, those are big but not outlandish promises. Making sense of the world is, after all, the magazine's core business. What seemed outlandish, though, is the fact that the magazine's venerable editors were embracing smartphones and speed—two cultural memes with which the very nature of the *Economist* seems at odds.

It felt strange to be able to read a briefing from the *Economist* on a smartphone, but not nearly as strange as it felt to see the president of the United States sitting for an interview with Zach Galifianakis on the comedian's show *Between Two Ferns*. Galifianakis's interview style on the show, described on his Wikipedia page, is a mix of "typical interview questions, bizarre non sequiturs, awkward product endorsements, and sometimes inappropriate sexual questions and comments." Sitting between two ferns with anyone, let alone Galifianakis, is an altogether odd place for a world leader to find himself or herself. And it was altogether odd for this same president to find himself being interviewed on YouTube or, more recently, in Marc Maron's garage for his podcast *WTF*.

There had to be a reason—just like there had to be a reason for the *Economist* to suddenly start to covet the kind of attentional real estate that can fit snuggly in its readers' inside suit pockets.

Maron, the comedian most recently pointing a microphone at Barack Obama, offers some insights. In an interview for *Slate* about his time with the president, Maron explained what was on everyone's mind: How did this interview even happen?

> *They reached out to us! Months ago. Apparently one of his staffers was a fan of WTF. When they reached out to us I was like, oh yeah sure. Then all of a sudden it was happening. I was like ok where do I gotta go? Do I fly to DC? I'll fly to DC to talk to the president. And they were like no. He wants to come to the garage. I was like THAT'S CRAZY. (Maron, 2015)*

Obama's team reached out to Maron. And Obama wanted to go to the garage. Between those two statements sits an entire narrative about the way mission articulation works these days. Read closely . . . This was not an example of a cult-status entertainer hustling for a decade and finally scoring the guest of lifetime, though he has certainly been hustling for a long time and Obama certainly was the guest of a lifetime. Maron did not do anything to land the biggest fish of his life—he just answered the phone—which means the big fish actually landed him. He didn't "catch" the president; the president's team saw a particular kind of media outlet, at a particular time, reaching a very particular audience . . . and they reeled it in.

Not so crazy, after all: Maron fit perfectly a digital strategy that the president had been using to flip the script on the way he tells his story and amplifies his message. He went to Maron's garage to work from a seething, hip, relevant technological platform that was barely a blip on the media landscape when he started running for president. He moved his agenda into a new technological space because such a move was a calculated bet that he could somehow deliver on his mission—that is, flex, extend, and reflect his mission—in a new or different or better way there . . . in that garage, with that comedian who has bled, sweat, and cried to assemble a passionate audience paying a very particular kind of attention to a very specific, hand-made, and social-media-enabled program.

The *Economist*, it turns out, plays its own kind of mission flexing, extending, and reflecting game when it moves its content online. Tom Standage, deputy editor and head of digital strategy for the *Economist*, gave an illuminating interview to Joseph Lichtman for the Nieman Journalism Lab in April 2015. In that interview, Standage was clear about what the *Economist* does not do. For example, they do not include links to external content in their stories. Standage explains, "[It's] not because we're luddites, or not because we don't want to send traffic to other people. It's that we don't want to undermine the reassuring impression that if you want to understand Subject X, here's an *Economist* article on it—read it and that's what you need to know" (Standage, 2015).

They can afford to be very clear about what they don't do because they are very clear about (and good at) what they do. They specialize in, chase, and deliver that "reassuring impression." As such, when they move their work online, they know which digital features to turn on and which digital features to avoid. They know which tools will help them to reflect their core mission.

The president, of course, is no different—only better. His own version of Tom Standage (Communications Czar Dan Pfeiffer) explained to Steven Levy why Obama's communication strategy has included stop-ins at online properties such as Buzzfeed and Funny or Die. Levy was sharp enough to call the article, "The Man Who Made Obama Go Viral." "Going viral" is not necessarily a term of endearment, since much of the content that goes viral is often quite trivial. And, do we really want to think of the president of the United States as content, let alone trivial content?

TRASPARENCY* IS NOT THE SAME AS CLARITY

JUST BECAUSE YOU CAN SEE IT
DOESN'T MEAN YOU UNDERSTAND IT.

*SEE CH.3

Regardless, the point Pfeiffer makes is that Obama's team, like the *Economist's* team, is singularly focused, knows what it is and what it is not. . . . and is willing to use technology to show its mission at work, to connect its work with new audiences, to reflect its missions more widely. According to Pfeiffer, "[They] simply couldn't rely on the same old mainstream communication tools to reach the public in the age of atomized media where people have a lot of choices" (Pfeiffer, 2015).

This brings us back around to schools, which face the same problem and the same opportunities. Eric Sheninger, a former award-winning principal and current senior fellow with the International Center for Leadership in Education (ICLE), has thought about schools in the same ways that Tom Standage has thought about journalism and Dan Pfeiffer has thought about political communication. Sheninger draws similarly pragmatic conclusions about the communication of school mission in his book *Digital Leadership*. "Societal shifts," Sheninger notes, "have made traditional forms of communication such as snail mail, newsletters, website updates, and even e-mail irrelevant as many stakeholders no longer rely on or value these communication mediums" (Sheninger, 2014, p. 78). His point is Standage's point is Pfeiffer's.

So what do we do? We do what we have been doing from the start of this book—take a close look at what blended leaders are actually doing in schools. There are plenty of fresh, bold, replicable examples of school leaders straddling the online/offline divide in ways that allow them to articulate the specific missions of their schools and the specific work that they do.

DAD'S OLD RADIO—FOR THE MASSES

About three years before this book was published, Todd Smith, an athletic director from New Jersey, started using Twitter to publicize the sports program at his school. The account has garnered more than eight hundred loyal followers since he first created it.

Like your father's old radio that allowed him to listen to baseball games while he chopped wood or checked the oil on his car (okay, maybe this was just Steve's dad), this account has allowed people from Todd's school community, or those interested in that community, to follow the important plays in the games of student-athletes as those games unfold.

A simple tweet brings you into the action of an important baseball game: "Cougars get the runner at 3rd. Runners at 1st and 2nd. 1 out." Two weeks later, Todd used the platform to showcase the achievements of student-athletes from the lacrosse team.

A quick look at the followers list for this account would show another benefit: The Twitter handle serves current students (hoping to keep up with their friends), former students (hoping to keep up with their alma mater), and local media outlets (hoping to "cover" newsworthy achievements in high school sports).

So how does this kind of thing happen? How does an athletic director build a following for a Twitter account? How does an athletic director—one person—create a sense of ubiquitous coverage when he can't possibly be at every game?

First, he publicizes the Twitter handle in a variety of ways. He tells people about it, follows them on Twitter, and even places it on T-shirts if that is what is needed. Second, he intentionally arranges the game coverage—not leaving anything, even the spontaneity of high school sports, to chance. Before games, he finds out which of his trusted colleagues will attend games that he himself cannot attend, and then he asks people to text him updates throughout the game. He then is able to post the relevant information to Twitter. He literally dispatches people to cover the games, and because people love the final product so much, they are glad to help.

Todd has always been interested in building school spirit and in building community in and around what happens on the fields of the student athletes of his school. Technology has allowed him to shift some of his leadership into an online mode, intensifying the way in which people engage with the athletic program he oversees.

And people are having more fun offline as well. Here is an email that was sent to Todd after one of the most exciting football games in his school's history. The game was played during the week, and the person who sent it was working at his desk:

> *Thanks for all the effort you make to spread the word about our athletics. I was following the football game on Twitter and I almost fell out of my chair as the game turned in our favor. I ran out of my office and bumped right into [another faculty member] who ran out of hers. Then we "watched" the rest of the game unfold on Twitter.*

Todd replied later that night:

> *I heard the Boys Soccer team gathered together in the locker room with their phones, and their parents had to wait 20 min. for them to get out. Heard the Field Hockey and Girls' Soccer teams were huddled around their phones the whole bus ride home, too.*

Without Twitter (or a similar social media platform), such community engagement could not exist. Without the smart phones that reside in the pockets of so many adults and students, such blended leadership, on Todd's part, is just not possible.

Antonio Viva, head of Walnut Hill School for the Arts, uses Twitter in an equally deft manner. We can see him tweeting about the success of an alum of the school:

Antonio Viva @antonioviva   25 May
Written by a .@WalnutHillArts alum ABOUT a
Walnut Hill Arts alum Via @nprmusic: Around The
Classical Internet: n.pr/...
Expand

Such success is important for people who attend the school—to see that others are "making it" in the art world. Also important to people considering the school is the quality of the teachers. Viva uses Twitter to showcase that quality, as well.

Viva routinely takes to Twitter to exhibit thought leadership in the arts, again an important indicator that his school is on the forefront of arts education. Viva also uses Twitter to highlight his school's strategic partnerships. If you're following him—as a current student or parent or a prospective student or parent—you are continually aware of the specific opportunities made possible by this school.

DR. GRAY SMITH REACHES FOR THE PNEUMATIC NAIL GUN

Robert Atkinson, founder and president of the Information Technology and Innovation Foundation, made an important point about innovation in a recent report from the Aspen Institute:

> *[When] it comes to what is more important to economic growth—more tools, a better ability to use them, or new tools—the answer is fairly clear. In building a house, for example, a pneumatic nail gun is more likely to increase productivity than multiple hammers or a training class on how to use a hammer better. (Bollier, 2013)*

We have said it before and we will say it again (and probably again): Blended leaders pick the best available tools to achieve the missions of their respective institutions. What we can add to that dictum in this chapter is that, at times, they adopt the right tool even if that tool itself falls outside their typical practice.

One of Steve's mentors, Dr. Gray Smith, recently became the head of an independent K–8 school in Maryland. When Steve met Gray, Gray believed in four things: education, lacrosse, fly fishing, and the power of a well-crafted sentence. Though he was very technologically proficient, Gray preferred the hand-written letter to any kind of communication that relied on social media. To this day, he still harbors that preference, but he started using Twitter professionally almost as soon as he was formally installed as head of school. Using Twitter had nothing to do with his love for, or comfort with, the platform. It was a leadership decision.

Gray's commentary on that decision, included in this chapter, surfaces the kinds of thinking that should accompany any move from offline or traditional communication channels to online, possibly trendier or riskier modes. Also, it sheds light on the decisions made by Todd Smith and Antonio Viva to move critical communications onto Twitter, as well as the way in which technology can help a school leader to reflect his or her school mission.

DR. GRAY SMITH ON TWITTER

I decided to use Twitter to keep our parents and constituents up to date on a daily basis about all the incredible things that happen at Harford Day School. Previously, we sought to do that through quarterly newsletters, sporadic emails, Facebook posts, and by word of mouth. With Twitter, I can capture something happening right here and now and send a great picture of it with a super-short description to parents and all our other constituent groups.

Traditionally, only the written curriculum is recorded, but the unwritten curriculum is just as powerful—some would even say it's more important, because it's what makes up the "magic" of the school. These are things like donut day in advisory, visiting your English teacher's horse farm during elective week, or getting into a debate about the Civil War with the Abe Lincoln expert history teacher. Twitter is great for documenting these aspects of the unwritten curriculum.

If you extrapolated the day-to-day routine [solely] from what's on our webpage, it would look pretty dry, pretty traditional, strongly academic, and it wouldn't tell you much about how we endeavor to have fun with kids while adhering to a culture that, frankly, is very academic and one that holds students to very high expectations for performance.

The biggest risk I felt I was facing [in moving some school communications onto Twitter] was that somehow the school's reputation would be damaged by a negative response to a post. Of course, I had to be judicious about what I posted as well, because I didn't want to inadvertently strike up a controversy. The rewards were letting our current parents and all of our constituents get a glimpse into the caught-in-the-moment "magic" of Harford Day School. Naturally, I also hoped to interest prospective families in the school.

I can't rightly argue that I used the Twitter feed to promote [my school's] mission. What I did was help people, internally and externally, see how we go about achieving it and that our methods are not—and never were—intended to exclude having fun, building strong relationships, trying new things, making friends, and being flexible.

The response has been entirely positive, which is always a surprise. I have parent and alumni followers who write back nothing but encouragement and tell me how happy they are to peek into this little window in their child's day or to say how glad they are that we still do, for example, the Medieval feast . . . a long- standing, unwritten curricular tradition.

I am just beginning to understand some limitations associated with Twitter regarding its facility for tracking data and for, subsequently, targeting Twitter feeds to demographically selected pockets of prospective families.

BILL STITES'S SOCIAL NUMBERS

Gray Smith's use of Twitter started with inquiry—"I wonder if this tool could help me show the day-to-day life at my school"—and it ended with a note of hard-won wisdom—Twitter is good for certain things but not for others. It is not a panacea; it has both affordances and limitations, and the skillful blended leader uses it just enough and in just the right ways—and then goes looking for the next version of a pneumatic nail gun. Gray will not abandon Twitter; he will even admit that "it's fun." But he will next go looking for a tool that can help him reach specific families and provide him with some data on how families engage with his communications.

Blended leaders know that one of the main reasons to tangle with technology is the data it provides; skillful blended leaders shape these data into compelling narratives. A good example of such practice comes from Bill Stites, blogger-in-chief for the increasingly popular edSocialMedia.com [ESM] outfit, which helps schools and individual educators understand and leverage the power of social media.

Some months, Bill sends out an email to anyone who has ever contributed to the blog. It is one of the best emails we receive regularly. Bill's energy and enthusiasm burst off the screen, sometimes pushing the very limits of syntax. You can tell that he loves representing edSocialMedia, and we have little doubt that his outright joy has contributed to the success of the project.

Relentlessly and enthusiastically pushing a project forward is an important component of leadership, as good and necessary offline as it is online. But we mention Bill's emails for their content—for what they can teach us about how a blended leader functions. In this case, the blended leader (Bill Stites) shares previously unavailable information, and in doing so, builds community engagement.

These emails routinely include what Bill calls "Social Numbers," that is, the number of "Likes" received from Facebook, the number of followers from Twitter, the number of members in the LinkedIn group, the number of subscribers from YouTube, and so on. He lists the current number and then notes the increase from the previous month. Why share such things? What do such numbers have to do with writing?

Right off the bat, Bill highlights progress, increase, growth; he makes momentum a tangible, graspable, witness-able thing. And then he continues, listing ESM's overall numbers, including the number of visits, the average time per visit, the bounce rate, the homepage views, the top ten posts for the month, and a list of the names, titles, affiliations, and contact information for any new contributors.

What starts to happen, month after month, is that the contributors not only share, but also feel a connection to one another. If, as a writer, you see your name in the "top ten" list, you know you have truly connected with your audience. If you are at a conference and you meet someone you have seen on the contributor's list, you have an immediate bond. Bill Stites's model is not only good for online organizations and leaders; it is also an emerging standard for all organizations and leaders.

BINGE WATCHING WITH JENNIE MAGIERA

If we are going to talk about the possibilities afforded by schools engaging with technology, we cannot simply talk about photos and data; we also have to talk about video making and video sharing. Jennie Magiera, CTO for Des Plaines, Illinois, school district and a former digital learning coordinator for Chicago public schools, offers some insightful reflections on the ways in which YouTube helped her to channel student creativity and voice and advance her district's mission.

As you read her reflections, you'll notice some common refrains—they came through in Gray Smith's thoughts about Twitter and they came through in other sections of this book. First, the technology sometimes shows different angles of the student experience or the school mission—angles that wouldn't have been observable without the technology capturing them and someone shaping them. Second, the blended leader is willing to disrupt the default, iterating based on what he or she learns in context.

Magiera started using YouTube playlists to "curate content to support and inspire student learning." She simply wanted to build a repository—almost like a digital textbook—to spark student learning. That was her plan, but her students had other ideas. "As time went on," Magiera writes, "my students were spending less and less time consuming and viewing content and more and more time creating their own original content. So my use of YouTube playlists shifted to showcasing my students' work."

Magiera's shift can be read as the digital equivalent of the sage moving off the stage. And once her students started to generate some shareable content, Magiera went to her default move for publicizing content: she started tweeting out individual videos. But Jennie quickly realized that, in doing so, she was bypassing one of the affordances of YouTube: "that YouTube-binge-watch phenomena where as soon as your video is over, another begins." In a deft move—borrowed from pop culture—Jennie created playlists with themes, encouraging viewers to "binge watch" her students' content, stay on the site longer, and extend the reach of the work itself, student work. As their audience grew, Magiera's students learned valuable lessons about empathy, authenticity, and responsibility. According to Magiera:

> *Having this diverse and ever-growing authentic audience has not only encouraged my students to continue creating, but also makes them more deliberate about their voice and message. They realized that when engaging on social media, you can't always control your audience, so you need to look at your words through more lenses. They began to more carefully craft their original content and made sure that if they said something, it was a message they truly believed in and said in a thoughtful way. (personal communication, June, 2015)*

Reshan decided to become an audience member; he sat down and binge watched one of the playlists. These are his running notes:

> *The first video is a submission for the #YesYOUCan White House film festival. The students who are on the screen share how they engage with their community and how they have optimistic hopes for the world. Coming from a school in Chicago, you can see their pride for the President running this program (a Chicago native, for a time).*
>
> *The second video is about coding. A different group of students present a dance and song about coding. The enthusiasm displayed is inspiring—perhaps to inspire other students to check out coding? These students are in middle school, by the way.*
>
> *Video three is another White House film festival submission—another original song talking about all the technologies they use. "It's a classroom and it's fun" is not something you hear from a lot of kids. Even more rare is the insight—again from the students—that they "learn better this way."*
>
> *Three videos in and not a single adult has made an appearance. It's all the kids.*
>
> *In video number 4, students defend their city. This video is different in that it is produced by the Chicago Sun-Times, and therefore scripted and produced. The audience, too, is larger. It is a response to a shooting and the way the media covers it, written and read by a 5th grade class.*

In the next video students image and prep android tablets for deployment. They set-up 25 tablets in 3 minutes. One of the devices doesn't set-up correctly, and one student walks through how to troubleshoot it.

Video six is Twitter Tuesday. Students talk about their Twitter sharing and interactions.

Overall impression: the students are confident and articulate. The videos are edited well. The tone is playful, but the messages are serious. It's unclear if this playlist reflects Jennie's mission as an educator or the school district's mission, but watching 10–11 videos from a single playlist immediately defines the school and its students. (Reshan, personal communication, June, 2015)

Students anywhere can create and post similar videos. And schools and teachers anywhere can facilitate a similar process for their students. What is different, and special, about Jennie's example is that she published these playlists from her own YouTube channel, therefore giving students unfiltered access to her own credible and wide network. She understands the power of networks to stimulate connections and learning; she understands, too, that she does not need to be involved, or visibly involved, once she combines stream A (her personal network) with stream B (her students' work). The benefits will flow freely as the two streams become one. Stream A will learn from Jennie's students, be inspired, and perhaps try a similar project at their own schools or places of employment. Stream B will gain an audience that Jennie carefully constructed and that understands what she is trying to accomplish as an educator. Like Tom Holt, mentioned in Belief 3, the master isn't burdened. The master, in fact, is out of the picture, allowing learning, growth, and development to flourish at its own pace and in its own way.

This is a point worth dwelling on a bit longer because it touches on an important aspect of network etiquette. Through ambition, effort, and resilience, blended leaders build up personal networks of people and information (see Belief 1). When embedded in a workplace, with certain defined responsibilities, they will often be faced with the choice about when, where, and to whom they will provide access to these hard-won and carefully curated networks. A good rule of thumb is, a blended leader should open his or her own personal digital networks to aspects of his or her professional life when the network benefits will positively affect both sides. Ideally, the blended leader will neither gain nor lose as a result of brokering such a connection.

So, for example, Reshan and Steve both used their own, personal accounts to tweet about the Startup 101 project described in Belief 2. They opened their networks because they wanted to inform their own associates about the project so that those associates might learn from it and possibly try it on their own; also, Reshan and Steve wanted to expose the Startup 101 students to a particular kind of attention—one that might lead to additional, self-generated opportunities for them after the project reached its artificial close. Think back to the reason for President Obama to sit for an interview in Marc Maron's garage. He knew he would gain access to a particular audience. All networks confer particular kinds of benefits and particular kinds of attention. When publicizing the work of your own students or schools, you should make your own personal networks available or unavailable with that in mind.

TWITTER+SLACK WORK BECAUSE:

(1) THEY HAVE A LOW BARRIER TO ENTRY

(2) ARE RELATIVELY FRICTION FREE

(3) THEY LET USERS SET BEST USE CASES.

So does a lightswitch

and that's why we work with the lights on.

MICROSTORYTELLING: WORKING MORE VERSUS WORKING DIFFERENT

Let us catch our breath for a minute. As we did in Belief 2, we can hear our busy readers shuffling and sighing: "Every time we turn a page in this book," you say, "Valentine and Richards tell us we have to do more."

It is true, if you employ a blended leadership practice, you can end up "doing more." But you can also end up "doing different." More, in terms of articulating your school mission, would involve brainstorming, selecting, and capturing media or text; editing and shaping that media or text; producing that media or text; and, finally, endlessly, marketing that media or text. These activities—which result in short films, medium-length newsletters, and long periodicals, all of which need to be delivered—require teams of people and a great deal of concentration. To do them well, if they are not your primary function, you need to be willing to devote hours—on top of your regular hours—to your workweek. That is the definition of more.

Different, in terms of articulating your school mission, would mean working with the gaps in your schedule and adjusting your idea of a proper and usable mission-related narrative. There are entire blocks of your days that do not change, that should not change. There are the meetings, classes, and other school commitments within which you execute your primary function. But you shouldn't need to go "above and beyond them" to do the additional work described in this chapter. As these blocks bump against one another, cracks of time open up. With the right tools, and the right mindset, blended leaders can use these cracks the way some rock climbers use cracks in mountain formations—as handholds and footholds to help them steadily and creatively reach their goals.

So when it comes to reflecting your school's mission . . . if you can maintain a floating awareness of your goal, keep handy a quick and dirty set of tools, and remain willing to hop from crack to crack without too much forethought or afterthought, you can articulate your school's mission in fresh, interesting, and time-sensitive ways. And by time-sensitive, we mean time-sensitive for you, the storyteller, and for your audience, the story receivers. We call such work, when it pertains to mission, microstorytelling. That is, microstorytelling is storytelling in and from small spaces, gaining mission-articulation handholds and footholds in and from small spaces. We learned about this practice by studying practitioners—all of the above—and by doing it ourselves.

Very recently, for example, Steve was heading toward a difficult day—a rock formation the likes of which he had never seen before in his professional life. His wife was away on business, which means Steve was taking care of all the family details plus serving as a school administrator, English teacher, member of various school teams, and the coordinating editor of a publication of Columbia University's Klingenstein Center. What made this particular day even more challenging, though, was that it was the first day of a program, for which Steve was responsible, called May Term. This program involved the entire senior class; they would be interning, traveling, doing community service, forming a startup, and working on creative, self-directed projects; they had 19 days, so the project needed to begin with a palpable sense of momentum and excitement; Steve had no time to waste, and no time in which to waste it. He had to articulate the goals of the program— loudly, clearly, and vibrantly—from the start.

When Steve arrived at school, bleary already from getting his two kids up, fed, packed, and safely off to school, he had to interview a job candidate.

After that, he had to prepare for a class and two other meetings, then finish grading three papers, teach the class, run the meetings, and deal with any other small, unexpected fires that popped up.

As he went through the first part of his day, he felt a weight on his back that kept getting heavier and an unpleasant taste in his mouth. He knew this feeling—it was the feeling of unmet obligations. We've all felt this in school from time to time. But Steve had worked hard on the buildup to the May Term program, and now he felt that he was failing it coming out of the gate.

But then he had a quick realization while standing up to walk to his class.

He was expecting to do "more" in a day when no more would fit. He was thinking of telling the story of the program in a way that just wasn't possible—because he had at least a half-dozen other jobs. On his way to his class, he took the long way, stopping by the room where one of the May Term groups (Startup 101) would be meeting. He took out his smartphone, snapped a photo, and went to class. When he got to class, he made a note in his calendar to return to the room at the end of the day. He looked up from his laptop and started the day's lesson—right on time.

After class, he tweeted a "calm before the storm" photo with a hashtag (#mkamayterm). At the end of the day, he returned for his next "photo session," snapped five photos, returned to his desk, and tweeted the best "after the action" photo. He wrote a quick email to the senior class to congratulate them on their first day of May Term, told them a new hashtag was active on Twitter, and encouraged them to use it.

Steve remained busy throughout the duration of May Term, but he continued his microstorytelling efforts, joined by others who implicitly picked up the concept. Some students took it upon themselves to chronicle interesting and candid moments. Teachers shared what they heard and saw. In season, Steve knew he would never have time to do the kind of thorough storytelling that he wanted to do; he knew he wouldn't have time to do any kind of concentrated writing, any kind of careful selection of the perfect, luminous detail. He would only have the briefest, barest access to the mechanics of narrative: the before-and-after, the surprise, the half blurry, the lunge, the grab, the quick triumph. He could settle for microstories or nothing at all . . . and in the end, microstories ended up being highly compelling. Ask any fans of comic books and they will tell you that comic book artists do just fine with constraints. If we think of mission articulation in those terms—rather than in novelistic terms—it becomes more doable. The longer stories can be written out of season, in collaboration with marketing departments, reflecting on the details that surfaced, looking back over Twitter feeds and poring through photo reels, knowing in advance already which details resonated with people.

In short, floating awareness of a goal, plus a smartphone, plus a willingness to jump from moment to moment (crack to crack), plus the faith that you will catch hold of something worth sharing is sometimes a good enough formula for reflecting your school's mission in the digital age.

MEASURING FAITH TO HAVE FAITH

The results of such faith, it turns out, can be measured. And, such measurement, rather than acting as a handcuff, can act instead as a spur to further experiments.

Let us look back to the previously referenced Tom Standage interview. Standage reveals himself to be a voracious learner on behalf of the *Economist*. His ridiculously clear sense of the newspaper's mission, along with his grasp of the company's shifting revenue streams, allows him to consider innovations happening in the journalism space and decide what his newspaper will and will not try. "That's a big thing that we're focusing on," he says. "How else can we apply the same values—which is the distillation and the finishibility, the trend-spotting and the advocacy—how else can we apply them to new areas?" (Standage, 2015). As they apply these values to new areas, keeping an eye on subscription numbers in both print and digital, the *Economist's* editors can watch the horse race of attention (and revenue) play out. Espresso, for example, is "up against lots of other products that are free. They're free, but are they sustainable? We'll find out" (Standage, 2015).

The "We'll find out" attitude is one that seems to drive Obama's team, too. Reflecting numerically on the president's interview on *Between Two Ferns*, Pfeiffer says, "We were able to track the people who clicked from the link at the end of the *Between Two Ferns* video, and it led to a huge spike in people actually filling out the applications to sign up for healthcare" (Pfeiffer, 2015). Other efforts, like a Facebook video breaking news about Affordable Care Act enrollment numbers, had only "a couple million views," which was "not as good as other recent content." Obama's digital team is able to take some bold risks because they know what they are trying to accomplish—their mission—and they have a set of baseline expectations to help them learn continually whether or not their efforts are paying off.

As such digital cycles become more refined, it is tough to know where mission articulation ends and mission advancement begins. What seems to be clear, though, is that broadcasting in a digital space one's mission, alongside reflections of that mission, drives organizations forward, upward, and onward. Eric Sheninger picks up on this concept when he talks about the importance of school leaders becoming "storytellers-in-chief"

(Sheninger, 2014, p. 99). He also helps us to unpack the relationship between such storytelling and the act of leadership, the act of driving and steering innovation. When such leaders use social media well, Sheninger writes, "a voice is created, stakeholders are engaged, thinking is shared, and consensus can be built for facilitating change" (p. 95). When we present our missions in vibrant and timely ways, people listen. They see a quick update on their phone as they ride the train in to work; someone emails them an article about an aspect of the school that interests them; their son is featured in an Instagram photo that has 100 likes; they want to get involved; they want to talk back to the school and share their own thoughts, experiences, observations, and examples. This process allows consensus to take hold and innovation to flourish.

The *Content Strategist*, an industry-leading publication for content marketing news and analysis, is in the business of tracking the way such communications can lead to growth in organizations. Tessa Wegert recently looked at the way three big players in the startup community—Uber, Airbnb, and Buffer—"fueled their growth with compelling content" (Wegert, 2015). Uber, a transportation company, produces a print magazine called *Momentum*. In it, they include stories from drivers and customers, helping to build Uber into a lifestyle brand for both drivers and customers. If you have ever taken a ride with a passionate Uber driver, or been berated by a younger sibling to use Uber instead of a cab, you know that the company benefits from such a strategy. Airbnb, a company that helps people offer, find, or rent lodgings, also has a print magazine. It is called *Pineapple*. According to its publisher, "This isn't a magazine about homes, it's about the connections that our community makes in the environments where they live or travel" (Wegert, 2015). Again, the content allows the company to articulate—and reflect—an aspirational component of its mission. Buffer, a social media company, meanwhile, specializes in "employee-generated content" via videos and blogs; they seek to express individual personalities within the company, show thought leadership, and reflect one of their most important "core values," which is "business transparency" (Wegert, 2015).

So there we have three big players in the startup world—a place to which we have been seeking clues to the potential future of our schools—looking to reflect their core values to either current or future customers or current and future employees. Each has a slightly different strategy with a completely similar purpose: to bind constituents more closely to the organization's mission. This, of course, is also the job of the school leader: to help all the stakeholders and potential stakeholders in his or her school get clear about what the school is trying to do; to articulate what the school is trying to do; and to allow that articulation to drive the growth of the school.

CAUTIONARY TALE #1: IF YOU DON'T DO IT, SOMEONE ELSE MIGHT

Regardless of how you feel about using technology to reflect your school's mission, you may not have a choice about whether or not to begin to own the online impression of your school.

Recently, we watched a professional organization with which we are affiliated undergo a major shift in leadership. When the new leader was named, a segment of the community erupted. For a variety of reasons, some thoughtful and some reactionary, some people could not believe the choice.

How did we know about their outrage? We heard the uproar on Twitter and various blog outlets. We scrolled through the diatribes, dialogues, rants, and reactions. Although we are not proud of the way some of our colleagues behaved, we did take one lesson from the fray.

The organization was criticized for not demonstrating openness and transparency (the same kind that helps Bill Stites to be such an effective leader of edSocialMedia.com). Granted, they tried. They set up a Web page and encouraged people with comments or questions to "send a note to an email address" or "use a Twitter hashtag." Good, right?

Not quite. The organization was then criticized for not permitting comments on the static Web page they had created. Because the organization would be receiving the comments via email, which is private, it is possible that they could cherry-pick the responses that they wanted to share or respond to, thereby controlling the discourse around their choice.

The possibility of this move—even if the organization didn't intend to make it—just doesn't sit well with people who have learned to expect the kind of open, transparent, nonhierarchal dialogue made possible by Web 2.0 tools.

Regardless of the organization's attempt at a forum, another forum was organized (by other leaders). They set up shop using a social network, attempting to pull together the conversation in an open and dynamic way. The conversation quickly generated more than sixty replies and nearly four thousand views, clearly serving the needs of the community: Some people needed to share information, some people needed to think out loud, and some people just needed to vent. In a world of connected computers, the leader is the person who enables the right kind of forum or platform to exist—whether it needs to exist for a long time, like the Twitter feeds of Todd Smith, Antonio Viva, and Gray Smith, or just a short time, like the one created after the shift of leadership just described.

CAUTIONARY TALE #2: PLAYING THE LONG GAME

In our first cautionary tale, we are not suggesting that you live in fear. But we are suggesting that you lead with your eyes on both offline and online spaces and an awareness, in particular, of the ways in which the latter can yield data and insights about how well your school is fulfilling its core mission.

In our second cautionary tale, we are asking you to hold a separate, and perhaps competing, idea in your mind. The results of education can often be seen quickly—a team can win a game, a hundred SAT scores can be averaged to understand the performance of a given class, a student can quickly pick up and apply a math concept. But the results of education can also be slow to emerge, and the game of education can be a long one, one that resolves itself many years after students graduate from your school. As you become adept at iterating quickly, at measuring more and more of your mission's impact, you also have to build the discipline to remind others—and yourself—that not everything that can happen in school happens during the timeline that school provides. Some of the best "measures" of your mission happen "off camera." They unfold internally in students—in the wild, developing, inner landscape of young people. And faster, when it comes to learning and school, is not always better.

As if to punctuate this point, one of Steve's former students wrote to him in the middle of the composition of this chapter. Steve worked with her more than fifteen years ago, at his first full-time job in education. Before receiving the email, he sometimes thought about the ways in which this student struggled, and he could only hope that she found her way.

She wrote to him upon receiving her PhD from a very prestigious institution and program. In her email, she reminded Steve that she had been a pretty mixed-up kid; she also reminded him about a moment when Steve pulled her aside and explained the way the school in which they both found themselves worked. He explained to her the different pathways available to students and encouraged her to take the pathway that would be most challenging. He saw in her a student who would thrive if she plugged into the most rigorous aspects of the school's program. She admitted to being "a bit miffed at the time," but also that this moment, where mission aligned for a teacher, a student, and a school, was a pivotal one for her.

The most important place for a school's mission to be "reflected" is within and around the student—whenever that student is most in need of it. Sometimes this will encourage a student to persist as a writer when his friends think writing is boring (that is what happened to Steve). Sometimes this will help a student to pursue his curiosity and his passion for music even when more practical concerns hone in on his attention (that is what happened to Reshan). And sometimes, like Steve's former student, this will help a mixed-up student (and what student isn't mixed up from time to time?) to buckle down, get to work, and end up becoming a scientist set on changing the world. In some senses, then, a school's mission can act as a protective layer, allowing the best parts of our students to flourish—when they are ready. This transformational process only works, of course, if all constituents know about the mission . . . that is, if someone articulates it loudly, clearly, and in the ways in which the constituents are most likely to see it and understand it.

An Offline Thing

Without looking it up online or in any other materials, write down your school's mission on a piece of paper to the best of your ability. Find a colleague or a team member and ask them to do the same thing. Compare your results. *Note*: If you find that thinking about school mission is tedious, or if you find that asking a colleague or team member to spend time thinking about school mission is not a good use of time, then it is worth a discussion about the role and presence, if any, of mission at your institution.

An Online Thing

Join a listserv, Facebook group, Twitter chat, Google Plus community, or any other space where other educators and leaders are active. If you are not sure where to start, search for #edchat on Twitter. Post a question or tweet asking people to share their school's' missions as part of your own curiosity around mission articulation. Create a document where you can save the text and links shared with you so you can quickly refer to it in your next mission-oriented conversation or exploration.

A Blended Thing

Set up a Twitter account or use your existing one if you are comfortable with it. Find the next major event happening at your school at which a large number of people will be attending in person, but just as many (or more) will not be there. It could be a school performance, a sporting event, or a guest speaker. Inform the organizer of the event and all of those performing that you intend to "live-tweet" the event, sharing commentary and possibly photos with the school community throughout. Inform your community two or three days in advance and then again on the day of the event. Attend the event (in person) and tweet your reactions and comments during it. Take some photos if you are able to and share them as well. Monitor likes, retweets, and follows. A day or two after the event, follow up with those who engaged with the live-tweeting and ask them about their experiences.

Photo by Justin Lynch

BELIEF #6

BLENDED LEADERS KEEP THE OFF-RAMP OPEN AND USE IT FREQUENTLY

NON-DOING SPACE

Last June, Steve was sitting in the back of a crowded room. It was the end of a long day and he had been called back to this room by a slightly inexplicable item on an agenda. Laptop on lap, he typed next to several other people who were also typing into some device or other. No one noticed the tall, lanky man walk into the center of the room until he cleared his throat and called the room to attention. It soon became clear that he would lead the final session of the day's meeting. Also, it soon became clear that the purpose of the activity he would be leading would be extremely unclear for most of the audience. His subject was the ancient practice of paying attention to a process that many of us take for granted—our breathing.

"In a few minutes, after some more explanation, I'll ask you to close your eyes—if you're comfortable doing so," he said. And then he talked to us about how we might sit and what we might do with our mouths (everything was couched in the conditional) and how it might be best to think of our thoughts, upon closing our eyes, if we chose to, as if they were clouds floating by. "You don't judge the clouds, right?" He didn't want us to judge our thoughts; he didn't want us to name our mental clouds "good" or "bad";" he didn't want us to be hard on ourselves if we could not focus; and he really didn't want us to work on anything. Being. That is what we were supposed to be doing in the non-doing space he had deftly and surprisingly opened up for us that day.

For Steve, this impromptu meditation session was the most surprising thing that had happened all day, all week, and probably all month. He had not signed up for this, and it did not flow logically from the event for which he had signed up. He was at his school's version of a tech conference. He had spent the day learning about Google Tools and backchanneling and Prezi and assessment. He wanted to try out the new tricks he had learned in a session on the latest Mac operating system (OS X Yosemite, at the time). He wanted, too, to respond to some emails that had been piling up. As he tried to settle into the guided meditation, begrudgingly at best, he spotted Reshan, who had engineered not only the tech workshops but also this closing event. He wondered what Reshan was up to. Was this some kind of elaborate hoax? An experiment? As he thought to himself, he heard another voice in his head, chiding him: "You shouldn't be pursuing that, or any, line of thought right now. The purpose is to focus on your breathing. The purpose is to stop focusing on the day's work, the day's screens, the day's technology." And then Steve knew exactly what was happening.

This meditation session was not solely, or even mostly, about meditation. It was about habits and default settings. It was a forced move away from hardware, software, and the networks that bind computing devices to other computing devices. Reshan wanted us to take a break—and not the kind of break that entails logging in to other social networks or email accounts to catch up on work between formal engagements.

The leader of the guided meditation said, "If your mind is filling up with thoughts, just let them go. Don't chide yourself. Gently return your focus to your breathing."

Steve agreed—still feeling a bit foolish—to give this a try. When he started to think, he returned his focus to his breathing. A few minutes later, when the leader called the people in the room back to attention, Steve felt refreshed, as if he had just returned from a dip in a cool stream. Maybe there was something to this . . . maybe.

get off the internet
superhighway —
regularly

leadership
nurtures
offline and
online worlds

HIGHWAYS AND OFF-RAMPS

Sometimes the first metaphor that helps you understand a concept frames your understanding of that concept for many years. For Steve and Reshan, one such metaphor is the "information superhighway." Not coincidentally, its Wikipedia entry identifies its widest usage in the '90s, when Steve and Reshan were beginning to hang out in educational technology circles. Listening to some of the ways it was used back then makes it clear why it would have been inspiring—in a "think of the possibilities!" kind of way—when we were in college and graduate school, beginning to inch toward our careers and our adult lives. Here's a definition, cited on the term's Wikipedia page, from an MIT working paper from 1994:

> *The information superhighway directly connects millions of people, each both a consumer of information and a potential provider. (. . .) Most predictions about commercial opportunities on the information superhighway focus on the provision of information products, such as video on demand, and on new sales outlets for physical products, as with home shopping. (. . .) The information superhighway brings together millions of individuals who could exchange information with one another. (Resnik, Zeckhauser, & Avery, 1995)*

So, with some sense of nostalgia—and because it has a certain utility to it—we are going to shake the dust off the information superhighway concept to help frame one of our most important beliefs.

We have celebrated the virtues of connected computers, highlighting and encouraging the way blended leaders travel the information superhighway in search of innovative practice. Along the way, we have tried to help you understand the leadership choices that are available to you. You now know, for example, that you can choose how and where to ask for help in a larger electronic forum and that you have multiple meeting options from which to choose when organizing the work of your teams.

But a truly effective blended leader knows that one of the most important parts of the highway, especially when traveling caravan style with a group, is the off-ramp.

Should you stay online or go offline? Should you take advantage of connected devices or disconnect? When leading others, what's the best way to mobilize them? Should they all be led in the same way? And what kind of moral responsibility do you have to a group of people—faculty and students alike—for whom you have provided technology and Internet access and encouraged robust use of both. If you're feeling as if there are many choices to make, you are on your way to being an effective blended leader. . . . Blended leadership, after all, is a growing awareness of the choices available to you.

LEADING OTHERS AS YOU WERE LED

Teachers, like all learners, learn in a variety of ways. Some of them like to figure things out on their own. Some of them like to learn by reading or watching. Some of them like to experiment and tinker with or without a "coach" looking on and offering advice. Some of them like to learn socially, in pleasant group situations that allow for them to move in and out of task focus. That this list could go on points to an important principle: If you ultimately want to blend your leadership, because you think that form of leadership is best for your organization or for the task at hand, you have to do whatever it takes to bring people on board. Sometimes this on-boarding is as simple as sending a group of people an email with instructions; sometimes it requires face-to-face work.

This point is not inconsistent with the way in which technology integration has worked in schools over the past fifteen years. Any nontech person who tried to collaborate with a technology department in the late '90s knows that the role of school technology departments have evolved quite a bit. As a teacher starting his career back then—if we can call working in a tutoring center at a college "starting his career"—Steve realized that there was a substantial divide between the people who were supposed to use computers to aid or ease instruction and those who were in charge of keeping those computers up and running. Back then, for Steve, tech departments were shadowy presences at best and gruff adversaries at worst.

Now, tech departments are often filled with people who are personable if not downright genial. Also, many folks who work on the technology side of things are often deeply invested in education and educational theory. They often know the language of education as well as, if not better than, most teachers, and they participate passionately in discussions about teaching and professional development. Somewhere along the lines (in the past fifteen years), school technology departments have internalized the idea that if we are to take seriously the concept that "it's not about the device," then the people who best understand the devices have to be approachable and approach faculties or individuals when need be.

The same holds true when blending leadership: If the device is simply a conduit to leadership, then the leaders who would use the device have to be approachable and approach those they lead when need be.

In our introduction, we urged you to take a step back and think about the first time you used Google Docs to collaborate. And we asked you to take a look at the online space wherein you post your assignments. We could have asked you to think about your initial engagement with Dropbox or Evernote. We could have asked you to think about the first few emails you ever sent in a work environment.

Our point, way back in the opening chapter, was that someone was "behind" those interfaces, those services. Someone outside your school made them possible, and someone inside your school decided to present them as an option.

Most likely, too, someone helped you figure out how to make use of them. He or she led your learning; he or she helped you become a more effective participant in an online world.

It is likely that, at some point, someone said, "Let me show you." You were in a meeting and the facilitator stopped the meeting to explain the tools the group would be using to collaborate. Maybe she went so far as to bring in members of the tech department to support the people in the room as they waded into an interaction on Google Docs or Moodle or Dropbox.

It is likely that, at another point, someone simply dropped you into a problem-solving context and asked you to figure out something for yourself. You showed up at a meeting and someone asked you to visit a website where the meeting agenda, resources, and notes would, from that point forward, be stored. But you were not totally familiar with the website so, as the facilitator ran the meeting, you had to try to pay attention to the meeting while muddling your way through a new online environment. Then, in between meetings, if you had an action item that required you to return to the meeting resources or notes, you had to figure out how to get back into the website. Slowly, all the clunky, laborious steps became fluid and habitual, so much so that you started running your own meetings through the website, so much so that you started leading the learning of others.

It is likely that, at even another point, someone invited you to simply play with something. You were working in your office and you received an email. It did not contain an action item or a complaint. It wasn't trying to drain what Seth Godin calls your "mental bandwidth." It simply said, "Hey, check this out," or "I saw this and thought you might like it" and then pointed you to something like Story Builder or Postach.io and you soon found yourself the proud owner of a new Web tool that you later applied to a presentation or a meeting or class.

And it is likely that someone, at some point, said, "Let me help you," and they came to your office and sat down with you and showed you, then watched you, then coached you, then showed you again . . . until you had it. And then they answered their phone—cheerfully—when you had a question. They continued to lend their support until you felt empowered to use a new tool on your own.

As you lead the learning of others, as you lead with tech tools and within tech-enhanced networks, it is best to have some examples in your head of your own experiences with similar tools and networks, or even better, online collaboration. It is best to think about how others have led your learning so that you, in turn, can lead the learning of your teams.

To be an effective blended leader, you must make conscious choices. Will my team use Google Docs, Moodle, paper, or some other medium? And does my team need tech support as we attempt to complete a task augmented by technology, or can we muddle through and learn as we go? In fact, would such muddling be most useful to the team, long term? Of course the answers to these questions depend on the tool, depend on the team, and depend on the purposes, both long term and short, of the leader.

Some teams can handle almost 100 percent online interactions and end up with an excellent final product. Some need offline interactions and support. You have to know your audience, drop in when need be, and always include the offer to meet one-on-one whenever something gets digitally ambiguous.

Reshan recently rolled out a new version of Moodle, with some small upgrades, to a large school community. In order to collect appropriate user feedback before pushing out the upgrade, he switched between online and offline leadership, as needed. For example, in a regular face-to-face meeting of his educational technology committee, made up of teachers, administrators, and librarians, he told the group he would be asking for feedback on the new Moodle space. He set the frame for the feedback by explaining some of Moodle's recent history at his school. The school's intranet, Moodle, had been in place for almost seven years with steadily increasing adoption and ongoing use. In the past, changes were made to Moodle in order to improve navigation and organization based on years of user feedback. Though visual design challenges had been addressed, access design was needed to make the entry into this space a cleaner experience. Moodle had been hosted locally at the school, which provided benefits (speed when it was working well, immediate support for teachers when needed, ability to restart the server) but also drawbacks (if complicated backend issues arose, the school did not necessarily have the local expertise such as an SQL database guru, to handle such problems). One possible revision to the access design was to contract a third party to not only host the Moodle environment, but also to maintain and support the back-end. The IT department worked with a company to create a site for testing so that people could see how it would work.

After providing the explanation to his group and taking questions as they arose, Reshan dismissed the group and told them that the rest of the meeting would take place online, and that he would send a prompt for feedback. He sent out the following message after the meeting, directing people to the test site:

> *Poke around on this site and see how things feel. I wouldn't get too fixated on the speed of things initially. I don't think that it is possible for it to be faster than the local solution, but at least it should be more reliable and not crash.*

So, he established the task in person and made sure people in the room understood what he needed. Then, and only then, did he send the digital communication with a restatement of the task and access to the online space. The digital feedback soon started rolling in. One committee member wrote:

> *I just spent a few minutes giving the new Moodle site a spin. I was surprised to see a few small changes. I don't know if the off-campus service is running a slightly different version of Moodle, but the look is slightly different. There are also two functionality changes that I noticed. 1. You can now drag and drop to upload files—finally! You can drag a file right onto your Moodle page and it will upload and make a title based on the filename. Or, when adding a file using the "add file" option, rather than having to navigate to the file, you can drag and drop it. 2. There is a new editing button*

next to each file/activity/page etc. that with one click allows you to rename the item (without having to enter the edit resource window). While neither of these is going to directly impact student learning, they will save time. The new Moodle server looks good so far!

Interestingly, Steve wrote this description of the Moodle testing in the previous paragraphs but was not at the original meeting. Reshan allowed him to participate by copying him on all meeting correspondences and all the feedback that came in. As an administrator, Steve was able to see the multiple layers that went into the unrolling of the next Moodle cycle, commenting if necessary. Because of Reshan's passive sharing, and Steve's willingness to engage completely online, Steve carried with him an enhanced understanding of the new Moodle interface—the ever-important backstory of the decision—when it appeared to the faculty and students. So, Reshan led Steve's learning in an entirely online way while leading the learning of his team in both online and offline ways.

If you spend all your time online, you will not lead as well as you could. And if you never pull back, and stay too involved, and never let the online tools take hold, you also will not lead as well as you could. To succeed as a leader with a blended practice, you must build the capacity for online–offline shifting.

THE HABIT OF WEARING YOUR HABITS LIGHTLY

And how do you do that? How do you know when to move a conversation or collaboration online or keep it offline?

Partially, the answer is obvious and intuitive: Do the obvious and intuitive work well. That is, as you lead, think about your teams and the individuals they comprise, keep your objectives front and center, consider the potential residual effects of any leadership tool or leadership path that you choose, and then make a decision about how you will lead.

But . . . the trick to doing that work well is to avoid rushing through it. If you always follow the same process, at the same time, in the same order, you are not deciding if that process is best. You are on autopilot, cruise control (on the superhighway). If you always meet with a team offline, for example, you could run into the problems detailed in Belief 4. Some members of that group will wonder why you never use the robust—and often free—tech tools at your fingertips to shorten meetings or cut out some face-to-face meetings altogether. At the same time, moving too much—or too quickly—into online spaces could alienate or isolate members of the team who are not comfortable working that way.

Being clear about your expectations while being flexible about the way you support others in their efforts to meet those expectations seems, to us, to be the best way to arrive at a situation that works. If you expect your teams to be able to use Google Docs in order to collaborate, you should be willing to say (1) Google Docs are now required and (2) I will offer you a menu of training options to help you feel comfortable using them. In order to make the right choice about whether to use the information superhighway or the off-ramp to accomplish your leadership goals, then, you have to develop the habit of wearing your own leadership habits lightly.

Habits are a vital aspect of technology use—beneficial when they create effective routines and dangerous when they reduce critical thought. When it comes to interactions with computing devices, everyone has habits and routines that guide their work, positively or negatively. Some people read the same websites, in the same order, every morning. Some people cannot walk past their smartphones without touching them. Some people read email continually during the workday. Some people need to be reminded to check their email (what they do with their time we will never know). Some people pick up the phone when others would walk down the hall, and still others would send a text or email. Some of these behaviors are useful; some are not. Additionally, habits are considered critical battleground states for technology companies hoping to be elected president of the world's attention. In an analysis on the blog "*Nir & Far*," Nir Eyal, author, consultant, and investor, says the "best product does not always win." To win, products have to "crowbar the competition's users' habits" (Eyal, 2015). Once a company has access to the habits of users, they have protected themselves, at least temporarily, against the advances of their competitors. This logic makes sense when you consider his examples. Netflix changed the habits of the Blockbuster customers who used to drive to the "video store" and even pay late fees when they forgot to return a DVD; Amazon put "the store inside the customer's home via the Internet," changing the shopping habits of millions of people.

Leadership habits around technology are just like all habits around technology. They evolve "slowly, then all at once" from personal experience (from inside of us) and from our environments (from outside of us). Some we intentionally build (the habit of exercising, for example) and some happen as a result of our crowded lives (the habit of not exercising, for example). To lead well, you have to ask yourself, are my online and offline habits optimized for the kind of leadership I wish to provide? Are they habits that I chose for myself, habits I stumbled into by throwing myself into my work without much thought, or habits that a technology company engineered for me?

When leaders acquire firm habits around the technology they use for leadership, they can speed through decisions, making their work seem effortless and decisive. Also, they can make mistakes. They might email an emotionally fraught message to a team—out of habit—instead of presenting the news in person. They might use old-fashioned, that is, slow, media to share news instead of social media, thus missing out on the chance to build momentum around an event as it is unfolding. They might reserve professional development for special speakers or summer workshops instead of trying just-in-time, peer-to-peer training or newer models like an "unconference." By developing habits and allowing them to continue unchecked, by developing go-to routines for solving problems or communicating, leaders can lose the power of conscious thought—they can lose the opportunity to exhibit judgment, to engender trust, and to build the capacity of their followers.

One way to avoid such a fate, and to wear your habits lightly, is to pay attention when someone starts talking about meditation and mindfulness (unlike Steve in the opening anecdote of this chapter). Google's Chade-Meng Tan's book *Search inside Yourself: The Unexpected Path to Achieving Success, Happiness (and World Peace)* chronicles the way an engineer brought meditation and mindfulness principles to Google. Tan's in-house Google course, according to a *Business Insider* report, has a six-month waiting list within the company. He teaches people—in the book and in real life—how to pay attention to their breathing. Also, and more important for a work setting, he teaches people how to process their emotions without acting on them in harmful ways. "We create problems," he writes, "when we are compelled by emotions to act one way or another, but if we become so skillful with our emotions that we are no longer compelled, we can act in rational ways that are best for ourselves and everybody else" (Tan, 2012, p. 18). What he calls "response flexibility" or "the ability to pause before you act" is similar to what we have called the "design pause" or "designing against the default."

As Tan teaches meditation to beginners, he offers subtle, easily generalizable counsel about what to do when you are meditating and you feel distracted. "If you have to react (for example, you really have to scratch)," he writes, "try to take five breaths before reacting. The reason to do this is to practice creating space between stimulus and reaction" (p. 42). We would say the same thing about the technologies that you habitually reach for and use as you seek to lead your organization. When you receive an input—that is, feel an itch to reach for your typical technological fix—take a few breaths; acknowledge what you are doing; open up a space, however small it may be, to choose either the typical, habitual path or something different, something potentially better or more human, given the context. Our leadership habits and default settings are too important to be taken for granted. They are too important to be set and forgotten. They are too important to be left to tech companies wielding better and better "crowbars" to loosen and grab our attention.

Boudett and City (we met them in our earlier chapter about meetings) help us understand what unexamined offline habits can cost us:

> *Our colleague Richard Elmore refers to time as "money you've already spent," which acknowledges that when you're paying people salaries, you're essentially paying them for their time. If you think about a meeting not as "60 minutes, but as $1,000" (for example, 25 people X 1 hour X $40/hour), all of a sudden the meeting feels a little different. (Boudett & City, 2014, p. 10)*

In his book on email, Mac expert David Sparks (2013) couches similar arithmetic in his typically lively repartee to measures the cost of an institutional online habit almost as common as the institutional offline habit of meetings:

> *Stop and think about it for a minute. Every time you get any type of momentum going with your work or, even worse, at play, that Ding goes off. What is the result? A rebellious piece of your brain disengages from whatever real work you are doing and thinks that it may be the most important email in the world. Like some Pavlovian dog, you then pull your phone out of your pocket or switch windows on your Mac to your mail application to find out that you've been made an unbelievable offer for Dr. Funkenstein's Fancy Hair Tonic. At that point, you've successfully enabled someone creating spam on the other end of the planet to interrupt your work or play. Here's the corker: in five minutes it is going to happen again.*
>
> *Now think about the number of times that can happen in a day. By default on the Mac, Apple Mail checks your email every five minutes. On your phone, push notifications will do it more frequently, indeed with every new email. Let's just stick with five minutes to be conservative. A notification every five minutes means 12 interruptions an hour. Assuming that you are around computers or cell phones 12 hours a day, that is 144 interruptions a day. It gets worse when you start thinking in terms of weeks, months, and years. (Sparks, 2013)*

Sparks goes on to ask how one can get anything done or find time for enjoyment when there are so many interruptions per day, per week, per month, per year, and so on.

Steve and Reshan have had plenty of people in their lives make the exact opposite arguments about meetings and email notifications. Many of the best leaders they know would rather run a bad face-to-face meeting than a crisp online meeting. They believe that teams build culture best when they share physical space consistently. And many of the tech leaders they know feel that leaders who turn off notifications are taking the unnecessary risk of not seeing important and urgent emails as soon as they arrive.

We are not sure there's a right answer, a correct way, in either case, but we believe strongly that there is a wrong answer, an incorrect way, in both cases: avoiding choice or pretending it does not exist. Leaving on your email notification system when you are trying to do deep, thoughtful work is an invitation to being distracted from that work. That's a choice. Turning off your email notification system will mean that your email system is less air-tight, less dependable to others. That's a choice, too. Habits and routines can save you, and your institution, time. Just don't set them and forget them.

TEACH OTHERS TO WEAR THEIR HABITS LIGHTLY, TOO

Many schools like to describe their employees as lifelong learners. Technology, moving forward, will test this assertion continually and thoroughly, but not only in the ways you might guess. Sure, when forward-thinking instructional leadership meets effective and capable technology leadership, the presentation of new tech tools for teacher use and student use will rarely cease.

But this chapter isn't about the way we market new tech tools to our faculties and students or how ready they are to adopt those technologies. It is not about tech integration or training, because that is not the focus of this book. Instead, we turn our attention to tech integration's unruly cousin: obsolescence. Though it is true that there are always new tools emerging, it is also true that some of the tools upon which we come to depend—habitu-ally—change continually or even disappear completely. Blended leaders must be prepared to grapple with the effects of obsolescence on commu-nities of practice; they must be prepared to think about and manage through the demise of those online applications and services that have gained a user base within their schools. Sometimes you spend a lot of time getting people online, into a space, only to have to move all of them off.

Let us take an example that touches most educators. As adults, we have adopted email utterly and completely. We send each other notes, make requests, share pictures, organize events—all through email. We have bought into the system wholeheartedly and, in some cases, overwhelmingly. Our stu-dents, in contrast, have lost interest in this medium. They have email addresses, but that is not where they transact most of their business. When they want to communicate with someone, they text him or direct message her. When they want to organize a group, they do so via Facebook. Sometimes they give up on words altogether, opting to simply share photographs via Instagram or Snapchat. Blended leaders notice the possible disconnect here and begin to ask questions about the ways in which teachers and students can best communicate in order to spur student learning. Should the adults alter their communication patterns, or should the students be encouraged to build a habit of checking their email accounts at least once a day? Who should give up ground here? Which highway are we even on? Which one do we want to be on? What is the best way to form an effective learning partnership between students and teachers? The blended leader has to stir this pot, has to raise awareness about conditions affecting online interactions, and has to plan for the fact that even a communication platform as seemingly solid and ingrained as email could one day crumble.

In watching leadership and "follower-ship" in online spaces, we have seen people move through a variety of stances when obsolescence rears its head and people are forced to work in its wake.

Stance #1:—Resistance

People receiving the news, and being asked to adapt to a new feature or a new tool, often begin with resistance (or not wearing their habits lightly enough). They do not want to learn how to use a new tool, especially considering that they spent part of their time, months or years ago, learning how to use the old tool. In this stance, they might be overheard saying something like, "I can't believe they're changing everything AGAIN. Didn't they just change things last year, and the year before that?"

Stance #2: Enthusiasm

Over time, if the new tools are truly better than the old tools, these same people will develop some buy-in that may even be marked by enthusiasm. For example, if "they" removed the ability for teachers to create PDFs directly from copy machines at Steve and Reshan's school, the same people who initially resisted utilizing this feature would be the first in line to stage the coup.

Stance #3: Taking for Granted

Partially, this shift in attitude has to do with stance 3—taking the change for granted. Once teachers have built enough muscle memory around a tool, and once that tool has become part of their habits, they often forget that it was ever new. Like driving their cars without thinking about all the steps, they create the PDF instead of making sixty copies of a twenty-page handout, they post their assignments to a course management website, or they project their computer screen during class. They could not imagine working without these efficiencies, which once were new.

Stance #4: Fluidity (or the .0 Stance)

The blended leaders behind such changes have but a single stance—what we call the ".0 stance." They understand that most viable technological products are introduced as versions, rather than as fixed and finished products. Version 1.0 becomes Version 2.0 becomes Version 3.0, and sometimes Version 3.0 is then retired. As such, blended leaders always have to try to guess the next iteration of a product or service . . . and be ready for it to fall apart or disappear or incrementally improve. They keep their eye on new features and figure out which ones are worth adopting. They listen to feedback from users and go looking for fixes if patterns start to emerge in that feedback. They watch what teachers and students do in online spaces, and then find new tools to align with those actions and the aspirations they imply. They notice when things start to break, when they do not function the way they should, and they overhaul systems even though those systems might be beloved, or so ingrained as to be invisible, to most users.

We have already discussed Ning, which for a time became central to the professional growth process at our school. Leaders at our school invested a great deal of effort to move people into that space. We vouched for it and trained around it. As the changes in the Ning business model started to cause us difficulty in envisioning a future with the product, we made the very difficult decision to move our users to a platform we had built in-house and could more easily control and monitor. It took a very clear explanation, and some coordinated support, to move people off of Ning and into our new space.

Over the past few years, other online leaders we know have tried to move people away from Microsoft Word, have replaced trusted (and clunky) AV cords with wireless systems, and have worked on shifting faculties from reliance on DVDs to reliance on streaming video. Blended leaders never get too comfortable; they realize that when we work online, we are always working in an environment made of digital quicksand.

However, in this quicksand, the only way to maintain stability is to keep moving. Therefore, while you are trying to convince your team that it's a good idea to adopt some newfangled online feature, option, tool, technique, or platform, you have to keep in the back of your mind that you might be transitioning them away from this product or service in the future. As Marco

Arment, founder of Instapaper, writes in a tough love blog post called "Your Favorite Thursday Sandwich," "Always have one foot out the door. Be ready to go" (Arment, 2013). The other option is to give up on companies like Google who "could shut down Gmail tomorrow if it made business sense." Really, even Gmail could be shut down tomorrow. Google has made unpopular decisions, for business purposes, in the past.

In 2013, for example, they shut down Google Reader, causing a frenzy among loyal users and, reported somewhat tongue-in-cheek by Nick Bilton, "near tears" from companies that relied on the service to power their own operation (Bilton, 2013).

People had grown accustomed to this service that aggregated/ provided RSS feeds from a variety of news sites and allowed users to customize what they saw. No one paid to use this service—it showed up with a standard Google account. No one, from Google, told people to form habits around the service, but people did, in both their personal and professional lives.

When Google ended the service, people's rage proved that they took the service for granted. Their habit blinded them to the fact that they now knew it was possible, and preferable, to aggregate news in one place. That experience did not have to end; that knowledge of preference did not have to vanish. In truth, plenty of options exist, and a broken habit should never get in the way of a productive or wise behavior.

MORE ON VERSIONING

In this mini-essay, Reshan bring us inside the mind of the companies on which we rely for software. He provides a rationale for the relentless versioning that blended leaders must account for as they make decisions about the technology that will be deployed at their schools.

We abandon versions—or compatibility support—of software on certain platforms when those platforms seem to be abandoning them as well, despite the fact that a user base exists. Of course we don't love this. For example, the iPad 1 (no camera, older design) cannot run any of Apple's iOS versions beyond version 5.0. They are on version 8 and about to release 9. There are features that will not work on those early machines, and Apple has no intention of making a concession.

Our future enhancements of Explain Everything will not work on iOS 4. So, internally at our company, we experience tension as we create updates for newer versions of iOS. Making these options available to older versions—while possible—can become expensive to build and more expensive to support. Unfortunately, those who do not move on (that is, update their OS or upgrade their device) sometimes can get left behind.

As software developers we live with obsolescence because we are depending on the companies that make the hardware and platforms on which our apps can run. When these companies release something new, we are forced to make updates—so the app will run and/or so the app doesn't look out of date (for example, when IOS 9 comes out it will support multi-app viewing—two at once—and our app needs to be able to play nicely in that space).

So in one sense obsolescence keeps us moving forward and forces us to have some agility in our design process. We remain ready for new variables to be introduced while still sticking to long-term plans. We also pay attention to other players in the market, but we do not try to get ahead of them by comparing ourselves to them or diminishing those products. We do try to see if there are other problems we can solve in a better way because this keeps users in our app instead of needing to be in a bunch of different apps to solve their problems. Our "Swiss Army knife" quality is something unique to us, to a degree, and it evolved in response to the context in which our app lives.

To change gears a little, the danger for schools in not adapting to the "real world" in which their students live is that they can end up developing or sustaining programs and procedures that do not adequately prepare students for the actual lives they lead (rather than the ideal lives that schools sometimes imagine for their students). In schools, things take a long time to evolve, a long time to be researched, built, and measured. So it is difficult to convince leaders that change is needed.

Instead schools might take on a mindset of agility: that is, they might establish long-term goals that transcend time and culture, and near-term procedures to quickly adapt and change direction without compromising those long-term goals. The job of the leader, in an agile setting, is to help align those pivots to long-term goals.

At Explain Everything (which, admittedly, is a smaller operation than most schools), when something new is introduced and we have to ask the development team to put existing work on hold in

> *order to focus on one specific task that had not been part of their planning, we are ready. Everyone gets on board because the leaders of the company have already shown that such pivots serve the long-term goals of Explain Everything; they are not rash, self-motivated decisions. Such trust takes time to build within an organization, but the freedom to change direction rapidly in order to best pursue a goal is well worth the time and energy it takes to make it possible.*
>
> *Even Apple (which, admittedly, is a much, much larger operation than all schools) plays this game from time to time. For example, they recently released iTunesU 3.0, completing a transformation from a content delivery and curation platform to a two-way collaborative environment. Now, multiple teachers can work together on an iTunesU class. Students can create work and submit it to a teacher or share it with a class. Teachers can provide feedback. When iTunesU was first released, I do not think Apple's intention was to go in this direction. However, Google had been setting the tone in this area of the industry with their releases of collaborative tools and platforms (Google Docs, Google Classroom). Apple pivoted to include the collaboration aspect. So they are now a good compete because they listened and adjusted. Perhaps more important, they have demonstrated that they are agile enough to build a tool around what happens, and what is needed, in the classroom.*

SAMR AS THE ANTI-HABIT HABIT

Generally, we think that it is better to avoid quick adoption of acronym-based learning frameworks and pedagogical theories. Recently, however, the SAMR model has been making the rounds in educational technology, and its simple presentation makes it seem accessible, sensible, and at the very least worth a look. It is not a brand-new approach to examining technology integration—there are many parallels to earlier work of Susan Loucks and Mark Prensky. Developed by Dr. Ruben Puentedura, it describes four stages of integration: Substitution, Augmentation, Modification, and Redefinition. A potential misconception is that one somehow has to move through these stages incrementally—that is, work from substitution toward redefinition. However, this model does not have to be used in an integration framework or pedagogical continuum. Instead, it can be used as an assessment lens or grounding diagnostic to define the types of interactions that are happening

in a learning, and therefore leading, environment. The SAMR model is certainly useful for tech integration, but it is also useful for blended leaders looking to adopt a .0 mindset.

If someone in your community introduces a new tool and people are just using it for substitution, then they can get hooked on it, and when it disappears, they will be lost. Leaders with a blended orientation will remind people to have "one foot out the door" by staying focused on what they are trying to do, rather than on the tools they are using. For if they are using the tools to redesign tasks, then, by definition, they will continually seek a different or better task (and quite possibly, a different or better tool, though the tool won't matter as much).

Collaboration is a good example. In work cultures where people have fully bought into the type of collaboration made possible by connected computers, there is a continual task-shifting based on the goals of the collaboration. If people want to work together in real time, they might opt for Google Docs. If they are archiving the work of a team over a long period of time, they might opt for Evernote shared notebooks. If they need a quick answer to something on which they are working, they might reach out and tap the digital shoulder of a person by texting or IM-ing or calling him or her. The task drives the tool selection, not vice versa. As such, if any of the tools mentioned here were to disappear or change significantly, the collaborators would still have their task in clear sight—they would still be working in ways that they hadn't been a year ago. They would simply find new, and they hope better, tools.

During the final year of his first three-year stint in teaching, Reshan was starting to understand his interest in educational technology and design. It was the 2002–03 school year, and he was excited about creating his own math resource webpage. Using the "Split Design/HTML" view in Macromedia Dreamweaver MX, he inserted buttons and animations that he had learned to create in a Macromedia Flash MX workshop. At the time, in order to create a webpage that looked exactly how he wanted it to look and function exactly how he wanted it to function, these were the best tools available for someone with little to no experience working with interactive website coding or programming.

It would seem, then, that for a teacher in 2003 to be able to create a space like this, he or she would need to learn the skills associated with Dreamweaver and Flash. An educational technology integrator at the time might schedule workshops and trainings around the use of these tools, even though the mastery of the tools was not the goal. The savvy tech integrator or online leader would be interested in tools only as a means to create or access something that otherwise could not be created or accessed.

Fast-forward ten years and Reshan is now in the position to teach the younger version of himself, someone looking to present materials online in as vibrant and human a way as possible. The goals are the same, but the number of tools available to reach those goals has grown immensely. Yes, Flash and Dreamweaver still exist (now owned by Adobe, of course), but the younger version of Reshan does not need to know how to use those tools in order to create a custom website. He could use Weebly or WordPress or Wix, three examples of the many great, free website-building platforms currently available. Flash as a platform is becoming obsolete—not only because of the lack of a flash player on Apple iOS devices, but also because of the emergence of HTML5, jQuery, and other streamlined and integrated programming approaches that no longer require third-party plugins in order to view and access content. Flash used to be the gold standard for sophisticated websites. The learning of Flash programming used to be a key offering during tech workshops and conferences. Now a site that requires Flash seems old-fashioned.

The SMART Board is another high-visibility tool that is approaching obsolescence. There was a (recent) time when a SMART Board in every classroom was an indicator of a high-tech environment, even though students were still using the same old paper-and-pencil tools while the teacher wrote on the virtually projected screen. With the recent emergence of tablets (like iPads and Android devices), the touch interaction and direct manipulation afforded by a SMART Board (perhaps the most valuable aspect of this technology) are no longer only available to the person who happens to be next to it. All students can interact with digital content when a multi-touch device is in their hands.

Many tech integration specialists can probably tell stories of spending a lot of time supporting teachers in their use of SMART Boards—but they should not regret that time if they used it to teach teachers that the tools are but a temporary means to create or access something that otherwise could not be created or accessed. The tools will change; the aspiration driving the use of the tools should not. In the case of SMART Boards, that aspiration was to create activities in which students could actively engage, not to simply create opportunities for students to annotate and draw over their notes. Teach teachers to desire the former and they will not feel lost or betrayed if the school decides to stop pouring resources into SMART Boards or if the company disappears due to the emergence of tablets. Rather than the boat, the saying goes, you should dream of the sea. You beat obsolescence by staying focused on the learning objective and simply using the best available tool at the time to support it (wearing your habits lightly).

This begs a question. In Reshan's graduate school program, there was a long debate among the faculty and the students: Should introductory computer programming courses be a requirement for master's and doctoral students in a program about educational technology (presumably those training to be at the forefront of school leadership, online or otherwise)?

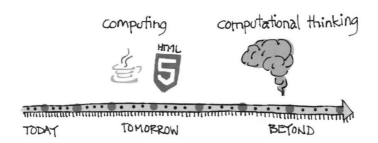

Reshan believed it should be a requirement only so that all students who are venturing into educational technology understand and experience what it is like to think and work like a programmer, considering that programmers are behind most of the tools that will be crucial to the graduate students' professional or scholarly work.

But when the conversation veers too close to the particulars—Should these students learn Java or HTML or Flash Action Script?—the general point seems to be lost in the scrum. Hidden in that scrum is obsolescence and all the havoc it can wreak if it is not a consideration in our strategic plans. All the languages mentioned here and their associated syntaxes are going to be obsolete at some point in our functional lives. No one who takes two semesters of programming in a graduate program for educators is going to be engineering the next Google just from these courses alone. Short-term thinkers worry about Java or HTML. Long-term thinkers worry about diving in and understanding what computer science affords by engaging as computer scientists. As described earlier in this chapter, when groups of people face obsolescence of a tool and the renewal that comes from it, they generally go through four stances: resistance to enthusiasm to

taking for granted to fluidity in the face of continuous change. In the best work cultures, a fifth stance follow the first four.

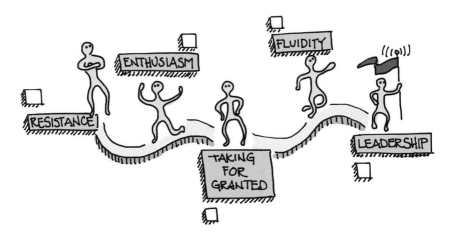

faced with obsolescence, people will take on recognizable stances. where are you?

Stance #5: Followers Become Leaders

Someone in this stance might say, "Things are changing around here, and they are going to continue to change because they are going to continue to get better, and I'm glad I work in a place that allows me to work at the cutting edge of my field." Once people reach this position, and find joy in the way their online work-life is elevated by continual improvements, they rarely go back to the earlier stances. Their whole approach has shifted.

In the fifth stance, followers become leaders. They are so attuned to what is possible that they begin to ask pointed questions, pushing their de facto leaders. You might hear someone in the fifth stance say, "You know, this program should be able to do more." Or, "This interface doesn't work as well as it should." Or, better yet, "I found an application that can replace the application we are currently using." Or, "Have you seen what this new X can do? Let me show you."

If leadership is working as it should, follower-ship does not get stuck in the early resistance phase. Change is communicated clearly. Habits are formed and reformed. Obsolescence, and the renewal it can provide, is occasionally contextualized and becomes part of the organization's vocabulary. A flywheel (in the Jim Collins [2016] sense) begins

to turn: As your faculty become used to incremental improvements in the online platforms on which they do their work, they begin to expect them. But their expectations are not marked by fear or dread. They look forward to changes, because they know that these changes are designed with their best interests in mind; they know that these changes are being pushed out by people who understand, intimately, how they work and the goals to which they aspire. They begin to ask for changes, in fact. They do not stay content with interfaces that lack elegance or require too many clicks to complete a task. They do not stay content when something does not work as quickly as it should. They understand that the online component of the school is as vital a part of the student experience as a common room or a classroom. They jump in to help train their colleagues, to share their insights, to promote an openness and a willingness to play, to explore, to sometimes fail, to be ever-amateur, in the best sense of that word. As such, by learning so fearlessly, they lead the learning of others.

THE MORAL COMPONENT

There is a moral component underpinning the belief expounded upon in this chapter.

If you are the one leading people into a deep engagement with the online world, you should remind them, from time to time, about the value and necessity of walking away from that world and the devices one has to peer into and bend one's body around in order to enter that world.

If you worked in a gym and noticed that people were overusing a set of weights, you would step in, cautioning them that they were in danger of hurting themselves or overdeveloping a set of muscles.

If you were a physical therapist and you saw people slumping in their chairs at their offices—for eight hours a day—you would warn them that their posture could lead to the deterioration of their body.

If you are blending leadership, if you are supplying people with new online tools, you should occasionally remind them to get off the machines, to leave the tools behind. As technological demands and possibilities increase, there must be times when technology is not around and is not used.

If you are creating professional development opportunities for your school, make sure you include some nontech offerings (like a giant group meditation).

Consider circulating something like the email charter (http://emailcharter .org) that offers guidelines about how we can use email effectively without drowning—ourselves or others—in it.

Consider promoting the message and practice of someone like neuro-psychologist Rex Jung, who suggests that "meandering" is an essential aspect of creativity. We swear we did not plan this, but he recently explained, via analogy, that intelligence "is a superhighway in the brain that allows you to get from point A to point B. With creativity, it's a slower, more meandering process where you want to take the side roads, and even the dirt roads, to get there, to put the ideas together" (Jung, 2015). So, as you structure work for your peers or direct reports, consider ways to promote meandering, whether intellectual or physical. Perhaps, at the start of a meeting, you can play a game like Disruptus, which encourages participants to rethink—and resee—everyday objects and ideas. Or perhaps you can suggest a walking meeting instead of a sitting meeting, helping to move a group out of its usual context, out of its usual thinking patterns.

If you are a leader, consider the timing of your emails. Do you send emails on Saturday and expect a reply? Could the email wait until Monday morning? Has anyone in your school told parents that they should expect replies to their emails in a reasonable period of time (say, twenty-four hours) but not over a weekend?

Do people in your school, especially leaders, talk about taking tech breaks? Do they ever post away messages on their emails that tell everyone in the community that they are unplugged every once in a while?

Online leadership that occasionally leads people away from their screens will likely become more crucial than ever. We are working at the dawn of Google Glass (and even Google Cardboard) and of machines that will be able to read and react to us, read and react to each other. Leaders will be the ones to say, "Thanks, yes, that's for us" or "Thanks, no, that's not for us."

TALKING WITH THE TECH RABBI

We move this chapter to its close by focusing on the life and times of Rabbi Michael Cohen, whose job asks him to stay plugged in to online networks more than most of us, while his spiritual vocation asks him to completely unplug once a week. He is director of educational technology at Harkham Hillel Hebrew Academy in Beverly Hills and a rabbi, and he joins his identities masterfully at his website, http://www.thetechrabbi.com.

We spoke with him in August 2015, and this is what he told us:

I am a full time educational technology director for a school. I have four kids, all five and under. I am in the middle of trying to finish my master's degree. I am also trying to create a consulting practice.

Once, over coffee, Scott McLeod [director of innovation for Prairie Lakes Area Education Agency in Iowa] asked me, "Are you going to burn out?"

I said "No, I have this thing called Shabbat." Every week I spend twenty-five hours totally disconnected [from technology], and I reconnect and deeply connect with people who are very important to me, especially my family and close friends. This practice gives me the energy to then go back to the online world and be productive.

It also helps me to think differently about what technology is meant to do. To ask, what is technology's essential purpose? My feeling is that technology, in essence, should connect us with one another.

I'm not insular, so to speak, but I've been very much in my little bubble in Los Angeles. After one opportunity to present at a conference, I've been thrust into the [ed tech] world. It's interesting to have conversations with people about what technology can do to better our lives and our learning. Then, never taking a break . . . I don't know how. . . I don't know what it's like to not take a break.

My weekly Shabbat is a humbling experience for me because it's bigger than I am. I think that sometimes when we use social media, it becomes a very self-centered activity. I don't mean that in a negative way, only that it becomes about the sharer. I think that the "bigger-than-myself" experience that I have every week helps me really understand that social media can be about a conversation—a meaningful conversation, a meaningful sharing of information. Though my Shabbat takes me away from social media for part of each week, it helps to shift and expand the center of things—including social media—for me.

We started this chapter with meditation and we ended with a reflection on the practice of the Shabbat. Though both are different, both are similar in that they help us to shift and expand the center of things—of a tech conference, of our social media use, of our leadership practice. What is all of this technology really for? Online or off, maybe that is the best path forward: asking that question, living the most thoughtful and thorough answer you can think of, and then asking that question again after some time has passed. Balance, in terms of blended leadership, is best thought of as a verb, not a noun.

An Offline Thing

Once a week, go for a walk outside. Don't bring your phone. Let someone know (or leave a note on your desk stating) the time you left, the direction you may head, and the time you expect to return.

An Online Thing

Start a blog to share your professional and/or personal passions and interests. Make it a priority to write something at least once a week. Block off one hour each week in your calendar dedicated to this priority. Automate your blog posts so that the links automatically get tweeted (or added to Facebook or to Google Plus).

A Blended Thing

Set a recurring weekly one-hour calendar event (daily if you can swing it) with a fifteen-minute alarm notification on your phone or calendar application. Make that time sacred (and "busy," as it will appear in your calendar). If something must get scheduled during that time, make sure you move this appointment to another time that same week. The title of this appointment? "Go offline." Use this scheduled time to walk around your institution, chat with people face to face, or just see what is happening. Don't bring your phone or computer. Imagine this time was an important meeting with someone during which you would not let yourself be disturbed. Bring a pen and paper to jot down notes or things that pop into your mind.

Photo by Charlie Foster

CONCLUSION

CONTEXTS

Good leaders have always shared attributes. They pull signals from the noise that each generation seems to encounter as overwhelming. They tell stories. They are brave and resilient. They organize people around a common purpose. They keep an eye on priorities and push their teams. They realign their teams when they get off track. They can be tough or tender, idealistic or realistic, strategic or tactical, as the need arises.

Though there may not be much new we can say about leaders, there is—will always be—more to say about the context in which leaders do their work, especially when that context changes dramatically.

The greatest athlete of his generation, Michael Jordan, had a great deal of trouble switching contexts (moving from basketball to baseball).

He could lead the NBA in scoring almost at will, but his stat line in minor league baseball was dismal. When he switched sports his physical attributes did not change, but his ability to apply them, to profit from them, certainly did. Our work, in this book and in the projects we have planned for the future, is designed to ensure that the leaders we most care about (school leaders) do not lose their touch the way Jordan did when the game he was used to playing—and playing well—changed.

To handle new contexts school leaders have to build new skills, new awarenesses, new sensitivities, and new habits. And they have to ensure that their new habits do not handcuff them to what will soon become relics from the past. The challenge is not overwhelming, but it persists and will continue to persist. School leaders must care about, and tend to, online spaces and the way in which teachers and students interact with, and within, them, especially as these spaces become more ubiquitous in and around our schools. School leaders must care about, and tend to, the blended experiences put forward by their schools, thinking of the online aspects of their school as carefully as they would think about a new wing of their school. We are not sounding a death knell for buildings in which school unfolds, just being clear-eyed about where much of school takes place now: online.

Much of the game—from the way people discover your school on a website, to the way that website helps them to deepen their understanding of your faculty and programs, to the way students gather educational materials, to the way in which teachers and students talk to each other and build relationships—is online.

Think about the last time you visited a website, let's say to buy something, where the interface really did not work very well. You could not figure out where to click to do what you wanted to do. There was no obvious way to seek help. If you completed a transaction, you did so in spite of the interface. Do we want students in our schools to have learned in spite of our online interfaces? To do high-level calculus in spite of . . .

Or, think about it this way. If, as a school leader, you walked into a classroom and found clutter, lack of clarity, a jumble of unorganized information scrawled on the board, a mess that obscured student learning, wouldn't you intervene? Would you not help the teacher? Why would you not do the same in Moodle or Blackboard or their equivalent at your school? Why would you not do the same in the case of poor email communication?

LIMITS

Blended leaders insist on a certain online presence for their organizations— that their organization's online presence be as good as it can be, as user friendly as it can be, as polished as it can be. They insist, too, that it improve incrementally, that it is maintained, that it is civil and reflects the best intentions of the institution. Blended leaders are the ones who care about the fact that people applying to your school cannot find what they need online, or that teachers have to perform eight different moves, six different ways, to upload a document to an online learning environment. They are the ones who say that an online resource could be more functional, more beautiful.

And they are the ones who, both understanding and respecting the online space, use the online space to connect with people, to build and maintain relationships, to learn, to save time, to construct knowledge, to be creative.

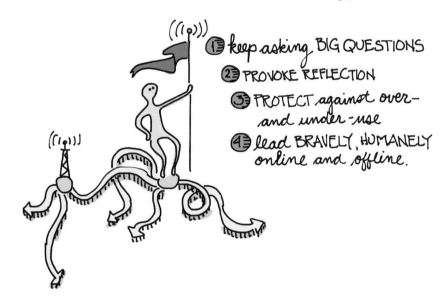

They use the online space to extend their leadership, keeping things moving in an age where a lot of people spend a lot of time reading on screens, staring at screens, touching screens, interacting with screens, and in fact, where a whole army of people, on the flipside, are devoting their considerable talent and energy to making those screens even more touchable, even more fun to play with, even more beautiful. As Scott Dadich writes in an article in the September 2013 issue of *Wired*, "the next great challenge for design" is "weaving the threads of technology, information, and access seamlessly and elegantly into our everyday lives" (Dadich, 2013). Fast forward to April 2015 to Farhad Manjoo's review of the Apple Watch in the *New York Times* and you see some of these predictions bearing fruit:

The Apple Watch's most ingenious feature is its "taptic engine,"
which alerts you to different digital notifications by silently tapping

out one of several distinct patterns on your wrist. As you learn the taps over time, you will begin to register some of them almost subconsciously . . . after a few days, I began to get snippets of information from the digital world without having to look at a screen—or, if I had to look, I glanced for a few seconds rather than minutes. If such on-body messaging systems become more pervasive, wearable devices can become more than mere flashy accessory to the phone. The Apple Watch could usher in a transformation of social norms, just as profound as those we saw with its brother, the smartphone—except, amazingly, in reverse. (Manjoo, 2015)

Blended leaders find a way to tame the complexity that ripples outward from ingenuity. Because of their own professional and personal networks, they hear about innovations more quickly than others. Because of their mindsets, they seek to understand these innovations before adopting them or abandoning them. And finally, because of their awareness of, and allegiance to, their organization's missions, they understand how to process innovations into existing systems.

So, to use the Apple Watch as an example: The blended leaders in your school heard about it first, understood it quickly, and knew right away that if it is as amazing at delivering covert messages as Farhad Manjoo says it is, it shouldn't be on the wrists of young people taking summative assessments or standardized tests.

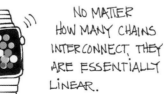

WE NEED TO UNDERSTAND HOW COMPLICATED TOOLS MIGHT HELP SOLVE COMPLEX PROBLEMS

complicated

COMPILICATED THINGS ARE MADE UP OF CAUSE & EFFECT CHAINS.

NO MATTER HOW MANY CHAINS INTERCONNECT, THEY ARE ESSENTIALLY LINEAR.

LEADERSHIP, LIKE ALL HUMAN INTERACTIONS, IS A COMPLEX PUZZLE. AND COMPLEX PUZZLES ARE NON-LINEAR

UM...

complex

Case closed—for now. For a restless blended leader, though, there is no saying that the Apple Watch needs to be permanently banned from teaching and learning environments (especially if its price comes down). They keep their eyes on new technologies, waiting for them to align with teaching and learning goals, waiting to see if such technologies will become better spurs to growth and problem solving than the ones their schools currently offer.

Blended leaders also look to leverage complexity—to see what new flowers can bloom in it. Give them Google Apps for Education (GAFE), for example, and they will begin by taming it, helping the community to build a common assumption that everyone in the community will be able to access— securely and privately—materials shared within the Google ecosystem. Once baselines for use are established, blended leaders will begin to leverage GAFE to generate outcomes that were not easily accomplished without it: easy-to-create Forms (for students) and automated spreadsheet entry (in Sheets) of the form results; collaborative presentation design (in Slides); easy website creation (in Sites); collaborative map making (in Maps), all with a very low barrier to entry.

Ultimately, blended leaders care most about the blending of the limited with the unlimited. Schools will always be artificially limited. They are rarely rich and they need to have clear policies and rules. But they should always also be inspirationally unlimited. Learning, in any given area, should not end simply because a grade has been levied. In the real world, learning begins after feedback, after evaluation, as resilient people ask, What should we do to respond? What should we do next? What should we do with what we learned?

Schools have to set limits. But, as Steve and Reshan are fond of saying, they have to set unlimits, too, for students, teachers, and leaders.

SPREAD THE SCREWDRIVERS AROUND

The last time Steve had a problem with his laptop, he brought it to a member of the school's tech department. Instead of taking Steve's machine into a secret room and returning it two or three days later, the tech handed Steve an OWC Envoy, a set of screwdrivers, and a new SSD (do not worry if you have no idea about the first and last items on that list; Steve felt the same way). The tech then gave Steve a few brief instructions about what to do, patted him on the shoulder, and said, "You can handle this. . . . Have fun."

Later that day, Steve sat down with his wheezing laptop, removed the screws, and peered inside a device that, in one form or another, he has used nearly every day for the past two decades. What he saw inside was . . . underwhelming. A few boards and circuits and wires. A few more screws. A band or two. He quickly did what he was told to do, popped the case back on, turned on the machine, and got back to work.

Weeks later, Steve's laptop is still humming along. It works the exact same way it did before it started having the problems that led Steve to bring it to the tech department in the first place. But Steve does not see it the same way; he is not working with it in the same way.

It is subtle and almost impossible to articulate, but now that Steve has disassembled and reassembled his laptop, he understands more of his own power as a user. He understands that the computer will do anything he tells it to do and that he can tell it to do almost anything he can imagine. Since that time, and for the first time, he has set up "smart mailboxes" and rules in his email, set up multiple databases to prepare for the upcoming school year, and set up a few recipes using IFTTT—"If This Then That," a service for automating tasks between otherwise disconnected applications. The tech who helped him to fish may have been in a hurry that day or he may have been acting deliberately (or, more likely, some combination of the two). Regardless, when he handed Steve the tools to fix his own laptop, he shifted Steve's view. He made him more of a programmer, more of a maker.

Education is buzzing about "maker culture," and for good reasons. Look around and you'll see tangible making via physical computing like Arduino or Little Bits or Makey Makey; fabrication like 3D printing and laser cutting; or simply the reemergence of the elements of historical disciplines like home economics (sewing, cooking) and shop (carpentry, automotive).

Then there is the digital side of making, which includes the software and screen-based digital tools to support tangible processes like coding a program in Scratch, designing a 3D model for printing in Sketchup, or drafting a mockup of a piece of furniture in Photoshop. Even Lego has jumped into the game, creating ways for children to build physical Lego creations and then import them into digital worlds.

But the idea of making and its relevance to schools is not new—what is new is that the entry point for accessing both the physical and digital tools and resources needed for making have grown as prices have dropped, user interfaces have been optimized for novices, and attention has shifted (or spread) back to thinking about "technology" as its own discipline (see the reference to the split of the strands in Belief 1).

So what should leaders do in this environment? Quite simply, they have to spread the screwdrivers around, to pick up the screwdrivers themselves, to help make or fix things that facilitate further making or fixing of things. Few activities are better for making learners, making leaders, or making makers . . . than making itself.

We believe that effective leaders are edging into this mode of thinking and are excited by it. As they lead, they make websites, Twitter handles, hashtags, auto signatures, infographics, slides, movies, and apps. They release prototypes, establish workflows, create models, and develop platforms. They fix fonts, straighten up shared tables, reduce clicks, share workflows, shed steps from those workflows, fix default settings that are bugging people, force updates with upsides when people are comfortable with the old version. They consolidate resources, move old online course material into new school years, write simple programs to eradicate collective headaches. They build partnerships with other school people and other non-school people. They hire sketchnote artists to represent ideas or learn to make sketchnotes themselves. They build . . . bridges . . . between people and people, people and machines, machines and machines . . . continually . . . in and out of view, and usually more out than in. They iterate continually, reflecting on previous prototypes, applying user feedback, and making the next version—of whatever they are working on—stronger than the last version. You will know you are in the presence of a masterful blended leader when the things around you simply work better, and you are not sure exactly why.

OFF ROLE

A shift in people's thinking comes when we stop associating roles with certain professions or contexts. Designers are in art school; leaders are administrators; learners are students and in school; makers are in workshops. Okay, but . . .

All humans are all of those things (designers, leaders, learners, makers). The key, we have found, is to realize the potential value of each role in different contexts and in knowing when to shift from one role to another.

Steven Levy recently resurrected a piece he had published in *Harper's* in 1984. In telling the origin story of the electronic spreadsheet, it explores both the difficulty and triumph of fitting round roles into square contexts. Dan Bricklin was in business school, doing his best to play the part of the aspiring businessman. But his mind kept bending back to the field of computer science, in which he had developed a deep proficiency at MIT and in two tech-heavy jobs. He was in the middle of an assignment for a finance course and he got itchy in the way that people who understand the power of computers sometimes do. According to Levy:

> *Bricklin knew that spreadsheets were needed for the exercise [and] he wanted an easier way to do them. It occurred to him: why not create the spreadsheets on a microcomputer? Why not make an electronic spreadsheet, a word processor for figures? (Levy, 2014)*

Of course, as Levy tells it, people told him he was crazy and that he should not be wasting his time doing something that could be handled in a different department or by someone lower in the hierarchy. Thankfully, he persisted, leading to a historical schism in the world of business:

> *[There] are corporate executives, wholesalers, retailers, and small business owners who talk about their business lives in two time periods: before and after electronic spreadsheets. They cite prodigious gains in productivity. They speak of having a better handle on their business, of knowing more and planning better, of approaching their work more imaginatively. (Levy, 2014)*

All of that because Bricklin was off role and yet decidedly on task. He was not procrastinating; he was spending time to save time. He was bringing a lacrosse stick to the basketball game, allowing him an unheard of reach and an unrivaled advantage. Levy captures the value of the venture nicely: "A brilliant model is not only beautiful, it yields insights impossible to attain by any other method" (Levy, 2014). Such models become common outputs of electronic spreadsheets, and Bricklin's story, too, becomes a model for leaders who understand the value of role shifting, of picking up an outside industry's tools to remake the tools in one's own industry.

Blended leaders do not feel a need to be technologists, but they are wired to be techno-curious. To have a technological bent in their thinking. To know that, if they don't continue to make or acquire new models, they will continue to see the way they always have, stymying progress and possibility. To know that, if a problem keeps popping up, or an opportunity keeps slipping past, that something can be built to make sure the problem never happens again and the opportunity always happens again.

PROFILES IN EXACTLY THAT

Have you ever heard of MinecraftEDU? Did you contribute to the Kickstarter campaign for Make!Sense? Do your colleagues and students use Explain Everything? Each is an innovation founded or cofounded by a practicing educator who saw and seized an opportunity to apply a technological solution to a contextual problem in his own practice. Each is a story of an educator who used design methodology, continual testing, and implementation in context to realize his ideas. Each is a story of a teacher and leader who shifted to a different role—maker, inventor, game designer—without ever fully shedding his primary role—helping students reach their full potential.

Minecraft is an open-ended design world with an active community of players and creators who bring their worlds to life. MinecraftEDU was started by Joel Levin after using Minecraft with his daughter and thinking he could bring similar excitement and deep creative and exploratory experiences to students at his school. Unlike Bricklin in the previous example, Levin found that his school's strong, forward-thinking, growth mindset-oriented leadership was willing to take a risk and try something new. Along with that, he found students excited about a gaming/learning experience, not fully realizing the skills they were acquiring as they were playing what they normally perceived as a game.

He then decided to start crafting his own worlds for Minecraft—worlds that could support and extend his teaching, learning, and blogging. Soon other educators were interested in his work, and he teamed up with some excited graduate students in Finland who were interested in studying Minecraft as part of their thesis research. They formed a company—TeacherGaming—to bring MinecraftEDU to the masses. Support from Notch/Minecraft (a company later acquired by Microsoft for ~$2.2 billion) followed, and they continue to share their work all over the world at conferences and trade shows.

Stephen Lewis once invented a clever tool—the Color Day Calendar AutoMater—for importing block and letter day school schedules into traditional calendar programs. A consummate inventor, he then created a new prototype called Make!Sense. As a science teacher, he found that probes and sensor equipment manufactured by traditional vendors were costly and often difficult to use. Also, the devices were not always forward compatible with new hardware and software. He decided to create his own set of low-cost probes that could plug into any device—a phone, an iPad, a laptop—and make authentic experimentation and data collection more accessible, more possible.

In order to raise the necessary funds to produce and distribute this invention, he started a Kickstarter campaign to fund enough prototypes to build and share with others who might be excited about the idea of low-cost scientific probes. He only asked for about $4,000, but he ended up raising almost five times that amount and was selected as a "Kickstarter Staff Pick."

Photo by Stephen Lewis

Always tinkering and trying to make new things, Lewis ultimately wants to help improve students' learning experience, and for him, this can best be done by making teachers' lives easier (through a calendar importer tool) and classroom activities more accessible and authentic (through Make!Sense).

Reshan had been interested in screencasting when he learned about it at a conference. Instead of simply using it to record his own lessons, he had students in his school record solutions to problems and then share those solutions in the class, with other classes in the school, and with a pen-pal school in Canada. The process was very rewarding for the students, and it gave Reshan interesting insights into how his students were thinking through some relatively abstract concepts. Unfortunately it was not an easy process to get going, requiring a lot of hardware and software, and it was not easily distributed or scaled. One setup per classroom, if that, was the norm.

Enter the iPad. An all-in-one device at a much more reasonable price point, it offered the same multiple hardware pieces (touchscreen board, microphone, computer screen) required to make a screencast. Unfortunately, though, the software needed to make screencasting possible did not exist when the iPad was released. While continuing to keep his eye open for such a tool, Reshan started an ed tech blog (http://www.constructivisttoolkit.com) where he wrote about iPad tools that were not necessarily designed for educational settings but allowed students to create interesting content.

One day he wrote about an app called PhotoPuppet made by two inventors, Bartosz Gonczarek and Piotr Śliwiński, in Poland. They wrote back to Reshan almost immediately after seeing his post, and soon after the three of them formed a working relationship. Many details in the story are skipped here (intentionally), but just a month later they had formed a business partnership, and a few months after that, Explain Everything, a unique screencasting interactive whiteboard was released for the iPad.

These three stories are unique and extremely relevant. They are the stories of educators who have crossed into the realm of entrepreneurs while trying to best serve the learning needs of students all over the world. They show that it is possible to turn an idea into reality by leveraging a network of people and information.

STEPHEN LEWIS AND HIS INVENTIONS

We recently asked Stephen Lewis to share more about his experiences and his work.

I've had a few careers. Right after Harvard I taught grade 4 for two years in Cambridge, and, inspired by my students' prosaic and imaginative work, wrote a photographic children's book called Zoo City, *which explored the idea that there are hidden animal images in city objects. Another book, some movies for Sesame Street, then a detour to get an MArch degree, in the middle of which, computer-aided design hit the field.*

I followed it, becoming an AutoCAD devotee and third-party developer. Inventions in hardware and software followed, a couple of patents, and then interactive software and toys. Finally I've settled into teaching and inventing, developing products for education and learning. The latest product is the Make!Sense series, which provides an easy platform for exploring physical computing. This one lives at http://www.makesense.co.

When the mysterious "six-day rotation" concept hit schools, it became quite a nuisance for teachers and students to figure out how to keep track of schedules that don't match the Monday-to-Friday rhythm that the rest of our lives follow. A hexagonal peg just doesn't fit into a pentagonal hole. So I cooked up a way to customize a database for each school's individual yearly and daily schedules that would allow teachers and students to enter their schedules for a single cycle, and then receive by email a data file, easily imported into almost any standard calendaring program, that correctly creates a calendar entry for every class meeting of the year. See it in action at http://nycischool.us/Scheduler/.

Everyone, including me, was tearing their hair out trying to enter schedules by hand. [The scheduler I built is] a pretty simple hack using PHP and mySQL. It's a one-trick pony, but it's a really good trick. I get tons of fan mail like, "I can't believe I lived without this," and, "You saved our teachers hours and hours of time."

The world of software and hardware production has radically changed with new design tools, available freelancers to help with complex stuff, offshore production, and simplified software environments. Ordinary mortals are able to see a need, create a solution, and just go ahead and make it themselves. You have to keep your expectations low, and hold on to your day job, but it's fun to invent and share the fun and productivity of new tools.

"BOTH–AND"

We are clearly enthusiastic about the possibilities for leadership in a new context. But, if you have read this book closely, you should have noticed a slight hesitancy at times. Blended practice is a "both- . . . and" construction. In our jobs and in our lives, we are quick to take three steps forward, but we usually end up taking one step back. The online world that we live in is, after all, eerily similar to the one Ray Bradbury wrote about in *Fahrenheit 451*.

In that fictional, yet prescient, world, too, screens were omnipresent. In that world, too, "screen time" was hotly debated, and at times, tied to status. If you had a flat screen on all four walls of a room, you were a digital elite.

We are not far off from where Bradbury said we would be when he wrote that people would talk to and interact with their screens (and would want to do just that), or when he said that people would be incredibly wrapped up in television programs—so much so that they would long to participate in them, to share their reality with the reality on the screen. In Bradbury's world, teenagers walked around with ear buds in their ears, rarely taking them out to experience the world around them.

And the teenagers also did awful damage to one another—they lost all sense of empathy. A kind of repressed brutality lingered just below the surface and sometimes reared its ugly head. People forgot how to be truly happy. What is worse, they forgot to even ask a question so simple, so direct, so fundamentally important: Are you happy?

Bradbury's book was published in the early 1950s. In September 2013, Louis CK, a philosopher-comic in the line of George Carlin, appeared on

The Conan O'Brien Show and delivered a bit/rant about why he does not allow his daughter to have a cell phone. Though it is a bit filthy in places, even with the television edits, it is also observant and profound (like much of his other material). He thinks that we rush to our screens (mainly our smartphones) whenever we feel sad and/or alone . . . and he feels that, by avoiding sadness and alone-ness, we sacrifice potential happiness, potential humanness. We lose the ability "to just sit there." He has a point.

And it is also worth stating that he had a point when he cut against the grain of conventional online wisdom, selling his comedy show through a website without DRM (digital rights management). People could either pirate it and pay nothing, or go to his website and pay $5.

He made $1 million in a fairly quick period of time, defying the consultants and the businesspeople and the attorneys, while elevating the dignity of his audience and his art.

Louis CK understands online behavior and how to get his point across in an online world; at the same time, as he pointed out in his cell phone rant, he understands the dangers of excessive reliance on that same online space, and he understands the ways in which online behavior might ultimately affect, quite seriously, our offline behavior.

Louis CK now, and Ray Bradbury before him, peered directly at reality . . . and saw that we share it with the technologies we create. He, and Bradbury, saw that the blended state of our lives has always been a problem, has always been an opportunity.

And, as has been the case throughout this book, the outside world leads us directly to a consideration of school, where enterprise is blended, too, where considerable problems meet considerable opportunities, too.

We have bounced between the words "*problem*" and "*opportunity*" to stress the importance of belief. When you look at a student or a colleague lost in the Internet during a class or meeting, do you see that as a problem ("Distraction is destroying us") or an opportunity ("I wonder if I can ask that person, who is so engaged with the Internet, to bring back some useful research for the conversation we are currently having")? When your email is overwhelming you, do you see this as a problem ("I hate email so I'm going to ignore it whenever possible, even it that further complicates my life or my colleagues' lives") or an opportunity ("I need to develop or research a better system to extract more value from all of these conversations that people want to have with me over email"). And when you talk to very young students (or your own children) about computers, what do you say?

Steve recently took a car ride with his kids. His son will be issued a laptop by his school next year, when he's in fourth grade, and on this particular ride, that computer became the topic of conversation. Steve started the conversation, innocently enough, by saying, "You'll get a computer next year, Hunter. That should be pretty cool."

Steve's daughter, who was four at the time, said, "Hunter will be a giant next year."

Hunter, in his way, responded to both comments: "The computer's mainly for homework. . . . And I won't be a giant. That's about six months from now. I'm not going to grow that much."

After a pause, he kept going with that idea: "Imagine that. I wouldn't fit in this car. Dad, we're going to need a new car if that happens."

And then more from Chloe: "You know . . . your heart is a muscle." They were doing what they do best, randomly associating and having fun, but I wanted to go backward in the conversation. I wanted to talk more about computers because Hunter's comment about homework had hit me like a punch. I cut in.

"That machine is for homework, sure, but it is also for other things. Like making stuff. And storing music that you love. And programming. And doing math. And keeping track of birthdays. And combining pictures with sounds." I was getting carried away because it seemed so important, at that moment, that my kids understood that computers are not just for doing homework, are not just for word processing, are not just for spitting information back to a teacher. "A computer actually *can* make you a giant!"

There was a pause and Steve felt his message settling in; he felt that he had been a good dad, a good educator, a good citizen.

"But then I won't fit in the car," Hunter said, and his sister and he burst out laughing and started talking about how they might need to use a saw to cut off the roof of the car if Hunter does become a giant.

So maybe Steve's point did not land with as much precision as he had hoped, but he is proud of the way he reacted, and he is happy with the set of beliefs that guided such a reaction. Our reactions, the way we respond to each situation, hinge on our beliefs. And our beliefs matter because they can shape everything from the way we pull a student or colleague into a conversation to the way we take responsibility for our communication practices to the way we help the youngest students (or our own children) understand the power of computers—and the gargantuan responsibility that emerges from connecting them.

Here is the thing we must not miss: Networkedness and onlineness make it impossible to be ignorant to the way others are living, make it impossible to avoid opportunities for empathy and understanding, without making a deliberate choice. When Reshan took a class on social and moral development at Harvard, he learned from Mary Casey (who studied with Carol Gilligan, who studied with Leo Kohlberg) that ideas around race and hatred of others that stem from no information and no attempts at empathy are culturally, and humanly, situated. No young person is born with those biases. The world around them makes such biases develop and stick over time.

The reason we digress on this point is that, with education generally, we have a responsibility—or opportunity to correctly address a responsibility— to educate and support the whole development of young people, rather than simply advancing personal ambitions, national goals, or societal norms. The stakes are larger now because the levers are longer: we should, and can, strive to advance and protect the human species. Kids need adults to bring them along until their brains are developed enough to make rational, independent, experience-driven decisions. Regardless of whether they are our own kids, the kids we teach, or the kids on the other side of the planet— they need adults in their lives who do three things:

1. *Establish norms:* Set goals and boundaries in order to prevent anyone getting hurt—physically, emotionally, intellectually—and to have a plan should such a situation arise.
2. *Provide access:* Open networks to people, tools, and ideas.
3. *Get out of the way:* Allow young people to develop on their own, at their own pace.

Do you remember Ahmad from our introduction? He was last seen asking Steve if he could survey his entire school to discover a problem to solve using his computer skills. He has assembled a small team and they are ready to get to work.

Do you remember the Startup 101 team from Belief 2? They launched their startup in May 2015. They graduated from the high school that sponsored that activity in June 2015. They celebrated with their families, traveled a little bit, attended college orientations, filed away their high school diplomas, and got back to work on their app. They were last seen meeting with administrators from their old high school, hoping to form a partnership that will allow them to test their app in a live setting.

These passions started in school, evolved half in school and half out of school, and, really, what's the difference?

What if domain expertise were less important than we sometimes suggest it is?

What if good teachers (and good leaders of good teachers) strived to develop a vast array of pedagogical strategies, a deep understanding of human cognition, and a contagious passion for their domain, not only enjoying the domain for themselves, but helping others to enjoy it for themselves?

What if some of our most cherished school practices were getting in the way of learning? And what if we found a way to tear those things down, to step aside, to hold the microphone for the students in order to amplify their voices, their understandings, their dreams?

Students are capable of much more than we can imagine. We do not control learning, and we should not seek to. We do not control all that kids can and do learn, and we should not seek to. We should, on the contrary, be wide open ourselves—to learning from anyone, from any source, from any amateur, from any student.

Blended leaders engage with and as thought leaders. They design and care for spaces. They reject insularity and embrace sharing. They challenge and change meeting structures. They articulate and advance missions. They keep the off-ramp open and use it frequently. They establish norms, provide access, and get out of the way. These are the practices that we believe will keep our schools most viable, most vibrant, in the twenty-first century.

Our beliefs evolved directly from our work in schools, our reflections on that work, our continuous conversations about that work, research we read, books and articles we read, and our observations of other industries attempting to thrive in the same cultural and economic conditions in which we find our schools. Our goal has been to describe school not as it was, not as it is, but as it is becoming.

We urge you to try on our beliefs to see if they help you frame your work (for yourself or for others) and to hold these beliefs up as "tests" for reality, perhaps via discussion groups. Are they accurate? Do they hold up in your context? Do they help you see fresh and new paths for your work? We realize that beliefs are not actions, but they can precipitate actions.

And so we come to the end of our book, which, of course, if the book is worth anything, is just the beginning for you. But also, in the connected world in which we find ourselves, this is just the beginning for you and us. What will we do with that insight, with what we can all do and learn together?

Photo courtesy of the authors

BELIEFS IN PRACTICE: THINGS TO TRY AFTER READING THE BOOK

An Offline Thing

Presumably, if you have gotten to this point in the book you have read at least one of the chapters if not all of them. Presumably, as well, there are at least a few points, moments, images, and/or messages that resonate with you, that you agree with, that you disagree with, that make you want to learn more, and so on. You may have made highlights or notes in the margins or marked pages with a bend in the corner or a mini-sticky note. Here is the final offline thing to try. Think of a colleague or a team member. Find five large sticky notes and find five pages in the book that you would like a colleague or team member to explore. On each sticky note, provide a question, a comment, a reaction, or any other leading prompt. Carry the book around with you until you see that colleague or team member in person. Hand the book over to him or her with the flagged pages, and ask that he or she spend a few minutes flipping through the pages you marked. Make a point to have lunch together the following week for a follow-up conversation.

An Online Thing

Access your Twitter account (or set up a new one). Compose a tweet that opens with "@sjvalentine @reshanrichards @blendingleaders: Hello!" You can leave it at that, or perhaps share a reaction or question right away. We will message you back, and, depending on the direction of the dialogue, may move it to other channels and spaces. We are excited to engage with you this way.

A Blended Thing

Provide a copy of the book to members of your team—one that you lead or one of which you are a participating member. Pick a chapter to read and unpack as a group and then, as individuals, select one of the three beliefs in practice at the end of the chapter to attempt over the next two weeks. Next, go to Google Plus, find Reshan and Steve, and send us a message. We'll coordinate a 30-minute Google Hangout where we can all discuss the reading, the ideas, and the results of your Beliefs in Practice attempts. We look forward to this connection.

REFERENCES

Ahmad, N., & Orton, P. (2010). "Smartphones Make IBM Smarter, but Not as Expected." http://www.columbia.edu/~na2189/files/T+D_Smartphones_Make_IBM_Smarter.pdf.

Altman, R., Stires, S., & Weseen, S. (2015). "Claiming the Promise of Place-Based Education." *Bank Street*. http://www.bankstreet.edu/occasional-paper-series/33/?mc_cid=3f484f0616&mc_eid=5f191d1bc0.

Andreessen, M. (2011, August 20). "Why Software Is Eating The World." *Wall Street Journal* (New York). http://on.wsj.com/1w2FbVs.

Arment, M. (2013). "Your Favorite Thursday Sandwich." *Marco.org*. http://www.marco.org/2013/03/21/thursday-sandwich.

Becker, H. J., & Riel, M. M. (1999). "Teacher Professionalism and the Emergence of Constructivist-Compatible Pedagogies." (Revised version of a paper presented at the 1999 meeting of the American Educational Research Association, Montreal, Canada.)

Berger, W. (2014). *A More Beautiful Question: The Power of Inquiry to Spark Breakthrough Ideas*. New York, NY: Bloomsbury USA.

Berkun, S. (2013). *The Year without Pants: WordPress.com and the Future of Work*. San Francisco, CA: Jossey-Bass.

Bilton, N. (2013, March 14). "The End of Google Reader Sends Internet Into an Uproar." *Nytimes.com*. http://bits.blogs.nytimes.com/2013/03/14/the-end-of-google-reader-sends-internet-into-an-uproar/?_r=1.

Bollier, D. (2013). *Power-Curve Society: The Future of Innovation, Opportunity and Social Equity in the Emerging Networked Economy*. Washington, DC: Aspen Institute, Communications and Society Program.

Bonk, C. J., & Graham, C. R. (2005). *Handbook of Blended Learning: Global Perspectives, Local Designs*. San Francisco, CA: Pfeiffer.

Boudett, K. P., & City, E. A. (2014). *Meeting Wise: Making the Most of Collaborative Time for Educators*. Cambridge, MA: Harvard Educational Publishing.

Bowkett, G. (2015, March 4). "Flaws in Scrum and Agile." *Panda Strike*. https://www.pandastrike.com/posts/20150304-agile.

Bradbury, R. (1967). *Fahrenheit 451*. New York, NY: Simon & Schuster.

Burt, R. S. (2001). *Structural Holes: The Social Structure of Competition*. In N. Lin, K. Cook, & R. S. Burt, (Eds.), *Social Capital, Theory and Research*. New Brunswick, NJ: Transaction.

Caylor, B. (2014, July 3). "Data for Web & Social Media for Higher Education." *Caylor Solutions*. http://www.caylor-solutions.com/data-web-social-media-for-higher-education/.

Chicago Digital. (2013, February 22). "Chicago on Github." *Digital Hub*. http://digital.cityofchicago.org/index.php/chicago-on-github/.

Christensen, C. (2014). Foreword. In M. B. Horn & H. Staker, *Blended: Using Disruptive Innovation to Improve Schools* (pp. xv–xx). San Francisco, CA: Jossey-Bass.

Collins, J. (2016). *Flywheel and the Doom Loop* [Video File]. http://www.jimcollins. com/media_topics/flywheel.html.

Covey, S. (2004). *The 7 Habits of Highly Effective People*. New York, NY: Simon & Schuster.

Criswell, C., & Martin, A. (2007). *10 Trends: A Study of Senior Executives' Views on the Future*. Greensboro, NC: Center for Creative Leadership.

Crotty, M. (2013, June 14). "Reflection after Hearing Paul Tough, Author of How Children Succeed, and Thinking about Failure." *To Keep Things Whole*. http:// tokeepthingswhole.blogspot.com/2013/06/reflection-after-hearing-paul-tough.html.

Dadich, S. (2013, August 13). "The Age of Invisible Design Has Arrived." *Wired. com*. http://www.wired.com/2013/08/the-age-of-invisible-design/.

De Pree, M. (2004). *Leadership Is an Art*. New York, NY: Doubleday.

Drucker, P. F. (1967). *The Effective Executive*. New York, NY: Harper & Row.

Duarte, N. (2008). *Slide:ology: The Art and Science of Creating Great Presentations*. Beijing, People's Republic of China: O'Reilly Media.

Ertmer, P. A., & Ottenbreit-Leftwich, A. T. (2010). "Teacher Technology Change: How Knowledge, Beliefs, and Culture Intersect." *Journal of Research on Technology in Education, 42*(3), 255–284.

Eyal, N. (2015, January 7). "4 Ways to Use Psychology to Win Your Competition's Customers—Nir and Far." *Nir and Far*. http://www.nirandfar.com/2015/ 01/competitions-customers.html.

Ford, P. (2015, June 11). "Paul Ford: What Is Code? | Bloomberg." *Bloomberg Business*. http://www.bloomberg.com/graphics/2015-paul-ford-what-is-code/.

Fowler, M., & Highsmith, J. (2001). "Manifesto for Agile Software Development." http://www.agilemanifesto.org/.

Fullan, M. (2011). *Motion Leadership: The Skinny on Becoming Change Savvy*. Thousand Oaks, CA: Corwin.

"Get Help with Economist Espresso." (2015). *Economist*. http://www.economist. com/help/espresso.

Graham, P. (2009). "Maker's Schedule, Manager's Schedule." http://www.paulgraham. com/makersschedule.html.

Greenleaf, R. K. (1977). *Servant Leadership: A Journey into the Nature of Legitimate Power and Greatness*. New York, NY: Paulist Press.

Gusen, C. (2014, July 24). "Managing the Unexpected." *Forbes India*. http://india. forbes.com/article/rotman/managing-the-unexpected/35381/0.

Hagel, J., & Brown, J. S. (2013). *Institutional Innovation: Creating Smarter Organizations to Scale Learning*. Westlake, TX: Deloitte University Press.

Hansen, M. T. (2009). *Collaboration: How Leaders Avoid the Traps, Create Unity, and Reap Big Results*. Boston, MA: Harvard Business Press.

Herb, J. (2013, January 8). "Display an #EdChat in Your Faculty Lounge—Instructional Tech Talk." *Instructional Tech Talk*. http://instructionaltechtalk.com/display-an-edchat-in-your-faculty-lounge/.

Hersey, P., & Blanchard, K. H. (1969). "Life Cycle Theory of Leadership." *Training and Development Journal, 23*(2), 26–34.

Horn, M. B., & Staker, H. (2014). *Blended: Using Disruptive Innovation to Improve Schools*. San Francisco, CA: Jossey-Bass.

Johansen, R. (2012). *Leaders Make the Future: Ten New Leadership Skills for an Uncertain World*. San Francisco, CA: Berrett-Koehler.

Jung, R. (2015). "Creativity and the Everyday Brain." *On Being*. http://www.onbeing.org/program/rex-jung-creativity-and-the-everyday-brain/1879.

Kane, P. R. (1998) "Farewell, Lone Warrior." *Independent School, 58*(1). http://www.nais.org/Magazines-Newsletters/ISMagazine/Pages/Farewell-Lone-Warrior.aspx.

Kaufman, S. B. (2013). *Ungifted: Intelligence Redefined*. New York, NY: Basic Books.

Levine, R., Locke, C., Searls, D., & Weinberger, D. (2001). *The Cluetrain Manifesto: The End of Business as Usual*. Cambridge, MA: Perseus Books.

Levy, S. (2014, October 24). "A Spreadsheet Way of Knowledge—Backchannel." *Medium*. https://medium.com/backchannel/a-spreadsheet-way-of-knowledge-8de60af7146e.

Lin, N., Cook, K. S., & Burt, R. S. (2001). *Social Capital: Theory and Research*. New York, NY: Aldine De Gruyter.

Manjoo, F. (2015, April 9). "Apple Watch Review: Bliss, but Only after a Steep Learning Curve." *New York Times*. http://www.nytimes.com/2015/04/09/technology/personaltech/apple-watch-bliss-but-only-after-a-steep-learning-curve.html?_r=0.

Maron, M. (2015, June 19). "An Interview with Marc Maron about What It Was Like to Grill President Obama" [Interview by Laura Bennett]. *Slate.com*. http://www.slate.com/blogs/browbeat/2015/06/19/marc_maron_interview_what_it_was_like_to_grill_president_obama_and_how_it.html.

McCain, B. E., O'Reilly, C., & Pfeffer, J. (1983). The Effects of Departmental Demography on Turnover: The Case of a University. *Academic Management Journal, 26*, 626–641.

McKeown, L. (2010). *Predictable Success: Getting Your Organization on the Growth Track—and Keeping It There*. Austin, TX: Greenleaf Book.

Miller, J. (2014, April 21). "Content Marketing: 9 Things Your Editor-in-Chief Does Every Day." *Scribewise.com*. http://www.scribewise.com/blog/bid/383344/Content-Marketing-9-Things-Your-Editor-in-Chief-Does-Every-Day.

Mintzberg, H. (2011). "Henry Mintzberg Interview." http://www.thinkers50.com/interviews/henry-mintzberg-interview/.

O'Reilly, C. A. III, Caldwell, D. F., & Barnett, W. P. (1989). Work Group Demography, Social Integration, and Turnover. *Administrative Science Quarterly, 34*, 21–37.

Parise, S., Whelen, E., & Todd, S. (2015, June 1). "How Twitter Users Can Generate Better Ideas." MIT Sloan Management Review RSS. *MIT/Sloan Management Review*. http://sloanreview.mit.edu/article/how-twitter-users-can-generate-better-ideas/.

Parker, I. (2015). "The Shape of Things to Come." *New Yorker*. February 23. http://www.newyorker.com/magazine/2015/02/23/shape-things-come

Pfeffer, J. (1982). Organizational demography. In L. L. Cummings, & B. M. Staw, (Eds.), *Research in Organizational Behavior*. Greenwich, CT: JAI Press

Pfeiffer, D. (2015, March 9). "The Man Who Made Obama Go Viral" [Interview by Steven Levy]. *Medium.com*. https://medium.com/backchannel/the-man-who-made-obama-viral-1c06bc3c8760.

Pinker, S. (2014). "Daniel Kahneman Changed the Way We Think about Thinking. But What Do Other Thinkers Think of Him?" *Theguardian.com.* February 16. http://www.theguardian.com/science/2014/feb/16/daniel-kahneman-thinking-fast-and-slow-tributes.

Poetz, M., & Prügl, R. (2015). "Find the Right Expert for Any Problem." *Harvard Business Review, June 2015,* 26–28.

Rainie, H., & Wellman, B. (2012). *Networked: The New Social Operating System.* Cambridge, MA: MIT Press.

Reagans, R., & Zuckerman, E. W. (2001). "Networks, Diversity, and Productivity: The Social Capital of Corporate R&D Teams." *Organization Science, 12*(4), 502–517.

Resnick, P., Zeckhauser, R., & Avery, C. (1995). "Roles for Electronic Brokers." In G. W. Brock (Ed.), *Toward a Competitive Telecommunication Industry: Selected Papers from the 1994 Telecommunications Policy Research Conference* (pp. 289–304). Mahwah, NJ: Lawrence Erlbaum.

Rheingold, H. (2014). *Net Smart: How to Thrive Online.* Cambridge, MA: MIT Press.

Richards, R. comment on Cuban, L. (2013). "iPads in Los Angeles and TCO." *Larry Cuban on School Reform and Classroom Practice.* https://larrycuban.wordpress.com/2013/06/21/ipads-in-los-angeles-and-tco/.

Rosenberg, S. (2015, May 8). "Shut Down Your Office. You Now Work in Slack.—Backchannel." *Medium.* https://medium.com/backchannel/shut-down-your-office-you-now-work-in-slack-fa83cb7cce6c.

Saffer, D. (2007). *Designing for Interaction: Creating Smart Applications and Clever Devices.* Berkeley, CA: New Riders.

Schwartz, T. (2013, February 27). "How to Be Mindful in an Unmanageable World." *Harvard Business Review.* https://hbr.org/2013/02/how-to-be-mindful-in-an-unmana.

Sheninger, E. C. (2014). *Digital Leadership: Changing Paradigms for Changing Times.* Thousand Oaks, CA: Corwin.

Sims, P. (2011). *Little Bets: How Breakthrough Ideas Emerge from Small Discoveries.* New York, NY: Free Press.

Sparks, D. (2013). *MacSparky Field Guide: email.* Orange County, CA: David Sparks.

Spreitzer, G., Bacevice, P., & Garrett, L. (2015). "Why People Thrive in Coworking Spaces." *Harvard Business Review, September 2015, p. 28, 30.*

Standage, T. (2015, April 1). "The Economist's Tom Standage on Digital Strategy and the Limits of a Model Based on Advertising" [Interview by Joseph Litcherman]. *Nieman Lab.* http://www.niemanlab.org/2015/04/the-economists-tom-standage-on-digital-strategy-and-the-limits-of-a-model-based-on-advertising/.

Stiegler, M. P. (2015). "What I Learned about Adverse Events from Captain Sully." *Journal of the American Medical sdociation, 313*(4), 361.

Tan, C.-M. (2012). *Search Inside Yourself: The Unexpected Path to Achieving Success, Happiness (and World Peace).* New York, NY: HarperOne.

Team Coco. (2013, April 16). "Louis C.K. Hates Cell Phones." YouTube. https://www.youtube.com/watch?v=5HbYScltf1c.

Valentine, S. J., & Richards, R. (2013). *Leading Online: Leading the Learning, Leading by Learning.* Ridgefield, CT: Constructivist Toolkit.

Wegert, T. (2015, April 16). "Story Hackers: How the Biggest Companies in Silicon Valley Are Using Content to Fuel Their Growth." http://contently.com/strategist/2015/04/16/story-hackers-how-the-biggest-companies-in-silicon-valley-are-using-content-to-fuel-their-growth/.

Zenger, T. R., & Lawrence, B. S. (1989). Organizational Demography: The Differential Effects of Age and Tenure Distributions on Technical Communication. *Academic Management Journal, 32,* 353–376.

INDEX